THE OLD IRISH OF NEW ENGLAND

A quick temper, a heart of gold, a sense of humor, and a gift of gab, mix gingerly with a rebellious spirit, a dedication to duty, a fierce pride, and a touch of creativity — and you have the proper ingredients to make an Irishman. Surprisingly, these ingredients seem to hold up, no matter how many generations separate him from the Emerald Isle. I have one Irish-American friend, two generations removed, who fits perfectly into this mold, so I fondly dedicate this book to him: Robert P. O'Meara of Salem, Massachusetts.

Bob Cahill confers with Jim Curley in Boston before writing this book.

Cover Photo: ISBN: 0-916787-09-5

Painting of John F. Kennedy on the beach at Hyannis, Massachusetts, by Bernard Fuchs, courtesy of the John Hancock Mutual Life Insurance Company, Boston, Massachusetts.

INTRODUCTION

During the Great Irish Famine of the mid-1800's, one-third of all Irish men, women, and children died of starvation and disease, one-third survived and remained in their homeland, and one-third, over three million people, flocked to America. Boston and New York were the main ports of entry, and by 1857 almost half the population of Boston was Irish Catholic.

Today, ten times as many Irish live outside the ancient motherland as live in it. In the American census of 1980, over forty million Americans identified their country of origin as Ireland. Over two million claimed that at least one of their parents was born in Ireland. Except for our nation's first settlers, the Irish were the first large foreign ingredient to be dumped into America's famed melting pot. Unlike many of the others, they were forced to migrate, and they didn't come willingly. When they arrived here, they were further persecuted by English-Americans, but it would be unfair to say that all "Yankees" gave the Irish a rough time, for many helped them to settle, find jobs, and learn. In Ireland, the English hadn't allowed them schooling, and they had a great zest to learn. Many New England Irish soon gained great prominence, especially in the fields of sports, soldiering, music, business, writing, and, politics. John Fitzgerald Kennedy culminated this one hundred years of struggle from the mid-1800's to the mid-1900's, by becoming the first Irish-Catholic President of the United States.

The story of the struggles and successes of the Great Irish Famine exiles and that of their offspring, is fascinating and inspiring, but even more interesting and less known is the story of the Irish who came to New England before the 19th Century. This little book is about them —, the Irish-American frontiersmen who came with the Pilgrims and Puritans, and who helped drive the British from American soil. The Irish were deeply involved in the making of America, especially when this country was in her infancy and started to blossom right here in New England. There is even more than a hint that the Irish were here before Columbus.

Over the years I have written a few articles on the Irish in New England, usually around Saint Patrick's Day for the North Shore Sunday newspaper— therefore, I thank North Shore Sunday for allowing me to use portions of a few of these articles.

I hope you enjoy reading these stories as much as I enjoyed researching and writing them.

Bob Cahill

1
THE FIGHTING IRISH

When I was fifteen years old and had played "hookey" from school on March 17th to join in the South Boston Saint Patrick's Day celebration, another boy about my age stopped me on Broadway. "You want a fight?" he asked, with no malice in his voice. "No, not today," I replied politely. He smiled and nodded with understanding and I walked on.

Sportscaster Howard Cosell recently admitted, "I was petrified of the Irish kids in my neighborhood when I was growing up. They always wanted to fight." Howard went on to say that, while serving as a major in the army, he bumped into one of his old Irish neighbors who was a private. "I was twice his size," said Howard, "and eight times his rank, but I still broke out into a cold sweat when I saw him."

Many football players break into cold sweats when they see "The Fighting Irish" of Notre Dame on their football schedule, even though only 25% of last year's team was of Irish extraction. In fact, Ireland herself is a mixture of many nationalities and always has been. Her shores have been invaded by foreigners more than any other country her size. Many of her conquerors, like the Normans who settled there, became "more Irish than the Irish themselves." Over the last few centuries, Danes, Vikings, Normans, British, Dutch, and French have entered Ireland en masse, and many remained on the island to become enmeshed in her society.

In 22 B.C., philosopher Polybius said of the "Celts": "In everything they attempt they are driven headlong by their passions, and never submit to the laws of reason"; Caesar said, "they are valorous and eager for battle": and Alexander the Great said, "they are of haughty bearing and great stature," adding that, "they are a vainglorious people."

The London Times once tried to characterize the "pugnacious" Irish by saying, "Ireland's beauty, warmth of colour and romantic wildness have reacted on the temperament of the people." British writer G.K. Chesterton tried to explain the fighting Irish in verse:

"The Great Gaels of Ireland
Are the men that God made mad,
For all their wars are merry,
And all their songs are sad."

American movie producer John Huston — who lived many years in Ireland — made films such as "The Quiet Man," and "She Wore a Yellow Ribbon," which depicted Irishmen as truly enjoying a good fight. "Yet," says Huston, "I have yet to see a fight, or even hear of one, in an Irish pub."

"I can lick any man in the world," boasted heavyweight boxing Champion John L. Sullivan, and when John L. was finally beaten, it was by another Irish-American, Gentleman Jim Corbett, who in turn lost the heavyweight title to a man of Celtic extraction, Robert Fitzsimmons.

Is it pride, one wonders, that sparks aggressive enthusiasm in an Irishman? It sometimes seems that Irish-Americans feel closer to, and boast more strongly of, the "Old Saud" than do the men from Eire. Even those of us who are two and three generations removed from the Emerald Isle, have an inexplainable sentiment for Ireland and those things Irish. British statesman Edmund Burke, an outspoken advocate of American liberties during the Revolutionary War, once said, "I love Ireland with a dearness of instinct that cannot be justified by reason." G.K. Chesterton called Ireland "an unhappy paradise."

Possibly the long British conquests and the terrible famines of Ireland, which forced our ancestors to come to America, have instinctively stirred the "motherland" blood in our Irish-American veins. During the American Revolution, a British general testified to the House of Commons that "50% of the American Army is made up of disgruntled Irishmen." This, of course, was an exaggeration, but Revolutionary recruiting lists show that approximately 38% of George Washington's Army was Irish born, or of Irish descent. The American Civil War also mustered a high percentage of Irishmen on both sides. After the battle of Fredericksburg, General Robert E. Lee said of the Union-Irish Brigade, "Never were men so brave." During the two World Wars, over 60% of those decorated for bravery were Irish-Americans.

Writer Max Caulfield may have summed up the fighting-Irish mystique when he said, "The Irish adapt well to terrible conditions and yet manage to retain a cheerful good-humored outlook." Or, possibly Lord Macaulay put his finger on the throbbing Irish pulse when he said, "Irishmen are distinguished by qualities which tend to make them interesting rather than prosperous." Actor Peter O'Toole explains Irish fearlessness differently. He says, "I think we Irish tend to react to what is expected of us, and overdo it at times."

Some modern day writers and philosophers think that intense religious beliefs, coupled with centuries of persecution, have developed Irishmen into slapdash and carefree martyr types. Yeats, one of Ireland's Nobel Prize winners, once said, "The Irish are men who believe so much in the soul and so little in anything else that they are never entirely certain that the earth is solid under their footsole."

Fear of further persecution may be at the core of Irish aggression, thinks writer Jack White. "The real fear of the Irish people is to be jeered at, to be laughed at," he says, "as a matter of protection, therefore, they try to be first with the jeer."

Besides loving a good fight, Irishmen and Irish-Americans are usually sensitive, fun-loving, patriotic, and gregarious. But, as poet Louise MacNeice said, "It is never safe to generalize about the Irish." It is therefore best to come to the conclusion that British Lord Gurzon did when he commented, "I do not understand the Irish. I know that I never shall, and that nobody else ever will either."

Archaeologist Jim Whittall stands beside an Irish Dolmen in Lynn, Massachusetts. Celtic Head found in 1941 at Great Chebeague Island, Maine. Sacrificial Table at Mystery Hill, Salem New Hampshire.

II
HOW THE IRISH DISCOVERED AMERICA

Few may know it, and many historians won't acknowledge it, but the Irish were here in New England hundreds of years before Columbus made claim to the continent, and over 1,000 years before the MAY-FLOWER deposited her seedy souls at Plimouth. The Italians, English, Spanish, Dutch, and Scandinavians, who claim that one of their own either discovered or first settled America, will - of course - be disappointed to learn this. Facts, however, refute their claims, and the history books will have to be rewritten.

Besides her warm people and cold pubs, one of the many fascinations of Ireland today, is her country-wide array of ancient ruins. Little round rock huts called "beehives", cave like chambers tunneled into the earth called "bothains" by the Celts, ring forts, burial mounds, stone megaliths, and tripod man-made monuments called "dolmens", pepper the Emerald Isle. Some were constructed by the Fir-Bolgs and the Tuatha De Danann, Celtic tribes that lived in Erin before the invasion and colonization of the Milesian Celts from Iberia, hundreds of years before the coming of Christ; others were built by Gaelic Druids and the first Christian monks.

My interest in the ancient Celts and their age old monuments, homes, and tombs, didn't peak in Ireland however, but right here in New England, especially at a place called "Mystery Hill Caves" in Salem, New Hampshire. Visiting Mystery Hill only a few years ago, I saw that the "caves" were not caves at all, but the same "beehives" and "bothains" that I saw and explored while visiting Ireland. The Mystery Hill caretaker told me that no historian, archaeologist, or anthropologist ever studied this half mile of rock ruins and man-made underground chambers until 1937, and that even then, it was by an amateur archaeologist named William Goodwin.

After a few years of digging and studying the site, Goodwin, a retired insurance executive from Hartford, Connecticut, concluded that Mystery Hill was once a Celtic monastery, built by Irish Christian monks in the 10th Century. Many professional arachaeologists disagreed with him. Some thought the stone structures were merely food warehouses constructed by colonial Americans, others thought the Indians had built them, and a few conceded that it might have been a Viking village. Although Indian artifacts have been uncovered at the site, most arachaeoligists today agree the Indians did not build the rock dwellings at Mystery Hill, and neither did the 17th and 18th Century white settlers. If they didn't, then who did?

When Goodwin uncovered a large rock slab with a deep groove carved into its edges at the site, Frank Glynn, President of the Connecticut Archaeological Society, recognized it as an ancient "sacrificial table" - with groves to catch the blood of sacrificed animals. The Celtic Druids were contantly offering up animals to a variety of gods, especially the sun-god, and even the early Christian monks ritualized the killing of animals for food. Finding the sacrificial table prompted Goodwin to write a book, "The Ruins of Great Ireland in New England," published by Meador Press in Boston, in 1946. Frank Glynn, however, after years of study, concluded that Mystery Hill was not an early Christian monastery, but the home of Bronze Age Druids, who somehow got to New England from Europe, possibly around the Third Century B.C.

Out of curiosity, engineer Robert E. Stone of Derry, New Hampshire visited Mystery Hill one day in 1956. He became immediately fascinated with what he saw, bought the site, and began a life of exploring, studying, and excavating there. Surrounded by his precious namesakes, Stone uncovered among other things, a stone shovel, and a stone carving of an arrow pointing upward and a bird with its eye and heart deeply cut into the stone for emphasis. The ancient Celtic symbol of an arrow pointing up, means "life", pointing down, it means "death". Birds and birdmen are prominent in Celtic symbolism, usually meaning reincarnation or life after death. The prominent heart probably stands for a person's soul or spirit, and the eye is usually the eye of God or of the sun. With a team of astro-archaeologists, Robert Stone discovered that many of the standing stones scattered about his 100 acres were actually astronomical alignment markers, monoliths carefully set in place to calculate the rising and setting of the sun, like those in Newgrange, Ireland, Stonehenge, England, and Carnac in Brittany. All three of these European sites were Celtic strongholds in prehistoric times. Professor Colin Renfew of the University of Southhampton, England, through carbon-dating, concluded that some of the European megaliths, or standing stones, were constructed before Egyptian Pyramids. Through radio-carbon dating of charcoal from fires, found two feet underground at Mystery Hill, Stone arrived at date of construction between 25 B.C. to 2015 B.C. The Newgrange, Ireland megaliths, burial grounds, and underground chambers were probably constructed about 2,500 B.C. Under one of the mounds at Newgrange on the River Boyne, is a 79-foot long rock walled passageway with three large rooms at the end of it. On December 21st, the winter solstice, the day after the longest night of the year, the sun beams directly into the passageway and lights up the three chambers which are completely closed off from the light every other day of the year. This has been happening at Newgrange, County Meath, for about 4,500 years. Mystery Hill is also an ancient astronomical laboratory, with monoliths used for solar and lunar alignments. The largest of these reflect the summer solstice, June 21st, and the winter solstice, December 21st, with sunbursts at their peaks. At the center of this astronomical and engineering wonder is where Goodwin found the sacrificial table.

Another remarkable discovery made by Robert Stone and Bert McKay, further convincing them that the ancient settlers of Salem were math wizards, was that the latitude of Mystery Hill is 42° 50.4!, and that of Cape Finisterre on the Iberian Penninsula where the Celtic Gaels departed en masse to conquer Ireland, is the same. This, of course, could be merely coincidence, if it is, it's a unique coincidence.

If the findings at Mystery Hill aren't enough to warm your Irish spirit or to stir your Celtic curiosity, there have been many more discoveries in New England - some of them quite recent - that prove our Gaelic speaking ancestors once lived here. At Lowell, Massachusetts, in LeBlanc Park, there is a 167-foot by 60-foot mound circled with tall standing stones, which are also aligned properly for the summer and winter solstices. It is theorized that Lowell's Stonhenge was constructed by 2nd or 3rd Century Celts. In Danvers, Upton, and Hopkinton, Massachusetts, Celtic "beehive" huts have been located. In the late 1700's, two boys chasing a rabbit, stumbled into a gaelic styled "both-ain" in Goshen, Massachusetts. Drystone walls and a slab ceiling covered with turf, concealed a 60-foot passageway with a chamber at the far end, like those at Newgrange, Ireland. The people of Goshen appropriately call this man-made cavern the "potato cellar". At Nahant, Massachusetts, overlooking the ocean, is a stone chamber with a slab roof ceiling, "similar to megalithic wedge tombs found in Ireland," says James Whittall, archaeologist for Early Sites Research Society. Nahant residents call their ancient man-made structure, "The Witch Cave," for, in 1692 during Salem's Witch Hysteria, two women accused of witchcraft hid out there. Only six miles away from the Witch Cave, on Lynn's Prospect Hill, stands a "dolmen" - a 70-ton granite capstone, sitting on three smaller granite "legs". "It seems to be erected with mathematical precision," says Whittall. In Ireland, dolmens are said to mark the tombs of great Irish Chiefs or powerful Druids. How ancient Celts, with no tools at their disposal, could erect such massive monuments remains a mystery. Another of these top-heavy, three-legged structures can be found in Salem, New York. Connecticut historian

John Williams of Danbury, identifies the New York dolmen as, "an ancient Celtic tomb." There is a dolmen at Bartlett, New Hampshire, and one in Kinnelon, New Jersey.

Three miles out of Stamford, Connecticut, in a soggy bog, are the ruins of 13 stone huts, thought to be ancient Celtic. In 1870, one of the last of the Stockbridge Indians, told the town fathers that through oral tradition, his people had passed on the story that the stone huts "were here when my ancestors came from the West." Writings in a cave at Ridgefield, Connecticut, have been identified by John Williams and members of America's Epigraphic Society, as "Ogham," the ancient alphabet of Irish Druids. At Preston, Connecticut, overlooking the Thames Valley, some twelve feet of ogham inscription was recently discovered, carved into a large boulder. A copy of the markings was sent to the headquarters of the Epigraphic Society in San Diego, and a dicipherment was made in August, 1984:

Ogham: ‖ ‖‖‖ ‖‖ ‖‖ ‖ | '|' ✗ \\ \\ | ✗ ‖
Decipher: G R N N G M F LA L L M EI D
Gaelic: Greine-ane   geim   fill   le   Meid
English: "The heat of the sun from winter returns at the Equinox."

Prior to the 1950's, it was thought that ogham script could be found nowhere but in Ireland or the Iberian Penninsula. Ogham monuments in Ireland number over 150, found mostly in the counties of Kerry and Cork in the Southwest. Not many years ago, archaeologist Robert McGhee found a large seaside rock in Newfoundland with ogham deeply scratched into it. He sent a copy of the markings to Ireland's expert in ancient gaelic, Professor David Kelley of the University of Calgary. He agreed with McGhee, "It is indeed Ogham." With this discovery and the uncovering of the "beehives" and "bothains" in various parts of Canada, Gustov Lanctot, Canada's national archivist, declared, "there is no doubt that Irish monks reached our shores before the Vikings."

Harvard professor Dr. Barry Fell, President of the Epigraphic Society, is New England's expert on ogham inscriptions. At Royalton, Vermont, not only have ancient cairns and subterranian tunnels and chambers been recently uncovered, but ogham inscriptions as well. Dr. Fell says ogham here is an early form, dating from about the Second Century. It wasn't until after 432 A.D., that Saint Patrick got rid of the snakes and Druids in Ireland, converted the Celts into Christians, and taught them the Roman alphabet. Fell, who is author of "America B.C." and "Saga America", deciphered Iberic markings at Damariscove Island, two miles off the coast of Maine. The inscriptions warned sailors that the island had lost its water supply. Also, ancient Celtic writing chiseled into a seaside rock at Monhegan Island, Maine, Fell deciphered as reading, "Cargo platforms for ships from Phoenicia." It is known that the Phoenicians traded with the Milesian Celts on the Iberian Penninsula as early as 200 B.C. Also, Iberian ceramic storage jars have been found underwater at Castine Bay, Maine and dug out of the ground at Bristol and Jonesboro, Maine, Portsmouth, New Hampshire, and at Boston, Massachusetts.

Two boys playing on Great Chebeague Island in Casco Bay, Maine, on September 4th, 1941, started scraping layers of moss from a large boulder and, to their surprise, a face carved with great care into the rock appeared. Two old fishermen reported that their grandfathers (who lived on the island) had told them about a carved face that had been found by the island's first settlers. "It is my contention that the Chebeague carved face was done by a Celtic explorer, sometime before 1000 A.D.," wrote Jim Whittall in a "Work Report" for the Early Sites Research Society. "The artistic style of the carving is similar to that of Celtic artwork", he concludes. A similar Celtic head, with an oak leaf and two acorns carved into its forehead, was cut out of a ledge at Searsport, Maine and is now on display at Sturbridge Village. Celtic Druids considered the oak tree to be sacred, and acorns as well as oak leaves were used for their rituals. A few years ago, an intricate carving in stone was found at Westford, Massachusetts, which experts identified as an ancient Celtic cross, dating to 1398.

The earliest Irish explorer on record, who sailed West in search of "the land promised to the Saints" some 1,400 years ago, was a monk named Brendan. He heard of a great land across the Western sea from another Irish monk named Finbarr of Cork, but how Finbarr got wind of it, we'll never know. With a crew of six men, Saint Brendan The Navigator, as he was later called, set out from Dingle Bay in a 36-foot skin covered sailboat, and he didn't return to Ireland for seven years. When he did arrive home, he told many fascinating tales about his adventure — in fact, a book, "Navgatio Sancti Brendani," was written about his voyage. It reads like an Irish fairy-tale — Brendan and his crew of seafearing monks encountered "mountains in the sea spouting fire," and "floating crystal palaces, monsters with cat-like heads, with horns growing from their mouths", and "little furry men." Their leather-skinned sailboat, or "curagh" drifted from one island to another, "following God's stepping stones," Brendan said, until he came to a large land mass — "The Promised Land", where he and his men lived for many months. He named this land "St. Ailbe". On their return voyage, they took a different route and ended up at the Azores; from there they sailed back to Ireland.

Some 900 years later, another famous explorer visited Dingle, Ireland to obtain information about Saint Brendan's voyage. His name was Christopher Columbus. The map that Columbus used when he sailed from Spain to the New World in 1492, had a large land mass located in the middle of the Atlantic Ocean. On the map it was named "St. Brendan's Island," but to Brendan, it was "Saint Ailbe."

A 36-foot leather boat, its sail bearing the ancient Celtic cross, left Ireland with six passengers in 1976. Her skipper, Tim Severin followed Brendan's "stepping stone" route to "the Promised Land". The stones were Scotland, the Hebrides, Iceland, Greenland, Newfoundland, Nova Scotia, and finally, New England. Severin realized that Brendan's voyage to Saint Ailbe, was the shortest route he could have travelled to cover 3,000 miles from Ireland to America. Today, it is also the air-route taken by transatlantic jets, because it's shorter than trying to fly directly from Shannon to Boston or visa-versa. But, if Brendan's Saint Ailbe was really New England, what about all those seemingly fictitious "mountains of fire, crystal palaces, cat-like monsters with horns coming out of their mouths, and furry little men?" Today, we realize that they were Iceland's volcanoes, giant icebergs, walruses, and Eskimoes.

Followers of Brendan in religion, seafaring, and exploration, were a large group of monks, most of them converts from pagan Druidism, called "Culdees". They originally settled in Amagh, Ireland, where they made their headquarters, and then fanned out throughout the land to spread the Christian word. In early 700 A.D., they were driven out of Ireland by marauding Vikings from Scandanavia. The Culdees sailed in their curaghs to Iceland and settled there, only to be driven out again in the 800's by the Vikings, who also wanted to settle there. Ari Thorgilsson, Iceland's historian in the year 1026 A.D., wrote that, "the Culdees disappeared from Iceland in a night, leaving many of their religious articles behind them." Thorgilsson also writes that when the Vikings colonized Greenland in 1007 A.D., they found remnants of white cloth and many religious articles, presumedly left behind by the Irish Culdees in their great haste to avoid Eric the Red and his warring Norsemen.

Two years later, 1009 A.D., Eric and some of his men decided to explore the waters south of Greenland. Thorgilsson gives us only a brief and spotty account of Red's journey south, but he does mention that during the trip he captured "two Skarelling boys who spoke the Irish".

They were on an island, and three of their companions escaped by "sinking into the ground." Probably into the long tunnel and subterranian chamber of a bothain. Eric named and catalogued the islands and lands he visited on his southern voyage, in this way: "To the south of Greenland, wild tracts, ice covered mountains, then comes Skarellings; beyond this, Markland, and then, Vinland. Near Vinland and inland, lies Albania..." "Skarelling" was the Viking word for "natives", and the island he called Skarelling, could be one of the Baffin Islands or Labrador — but most Viking historians believe he was naming Labrador. "Markland" means timberland, and was probably what we call today, Newfoundland. There is dispute to this day over what Eric called "Vinland", which could mean wineland or pastureland. Some believe he meant Nova Scotia, others have decided that Vineland is Cape Cod or possibly even Newport, Rhode Island, but no matter which it is, sailing "inland" to "Albania" — or as Brendan called it, "St. Ailbe" — would mean New England. Viking artifacts and writings have been found in Newfoundland, Nova Scotia, and Maine, and there is good indication that they sailed up the Merrimack River in Massachusetts, but what about the Irish Culdees?

Both Irish and Icelandic historians tell us that the Culdees always wore white robes, and constantly marched around carrying banners on long poles shouting and chanting, carrying holy books and bells with them. They are also credited as being excellent navigators, and had great knowledge of astronomy. The Skarelling boys who spoke Irish, captured by Eric the Red, told him that their people had no houses. Rather, they lived in caves or dens, and they wore white robes. They also said that they were ruled by two white kings named Avalldamon and Valdidia.

If, when the Irish Culdees disappeared from Greenland, they followed Brendan's route to Saint Ailbe and settled in New Hampshire, why would they travel inland, some 40 miles from the sea, at what is now known as Mystery Hill? To reach Mystery Hill, they could have sailed up the Merrimac River and landed at what is now Haverhill, Massachusetts, climbed Haverhill's largest hill, called Mount Washington, not to be confused with New Hampshire's Mount Washington, and they could have seen Mystery Hill from there, located only six miles away. Their reason for travelling and settling so far inland would be to avoid the sea-roving Vikings, who had already forced them out of three territories. We can further assume that their mission here, was to have the freedom to worship as they pleased, set up their astronomical laboratory, and convert the Indians to Christianity. It is intersting to note that when the French first landed in Canada, they were amazed to discover that the Indians there seemed to know more about Christ than they did, and even Christopher Columbus' most noted biographer, Charles Duff, admitted, "Celtic words were used by pre-European American Indians."

Even the name of the river that the Culdees would have had to manuever to get to Mystery Hill, although sounding like an Indian name, is actually Gaelic. "Merrimack" in Irish means "merry stream". When the Pilgrims landed in 1620, the Indians called New Hampshire and Vermont, "Coos". The Indians told the Pilgrims that it meant "crooked", for the rivers that flowed through the Northlands turned and twisted through the forests and mountains. In ancient Gaelic, the word "Crooes", meant "winding." Historian John Anderson, in his "Book of the White Mountains", published in 1930, writes that, "the story of Mt. Washington is the story of its apparent capitulation to the white race. The Indians shunned the mountain because the Great Spirit lived there, and they called it, 'Kan Ran Vugarty,' said to be Indian for, 'the continued likeness of a gull,' sounding to us, however, suspiciously Celtic." Even the names of some of our New England tribes have an Irish lilt to them; — names like "Micmacs" and "Mohicans". "Mohagen" in the Irish language means "untamed lowlander".

There is an old Indian legend, retold in John Spaulding's 17th - century book, 'Historical Relics of White Mountains." — An Indian hunter is lost in the New Hampshire forest in a thick fog. He hears noises like thunder, then chanting, and through the fog he sees, "a great stone church, and within this, an altar, where from a sparking censor rose a curling wreath of incense smoke. Around it, lights dispersed a mellow glow, by which in groups before that altar appeared a tribe kneeling in profound silence. A change came in the wind, and down a steep rock trailed a long line of strange looking men, and they disappeared into the rent rocks."

One wonders, could this old Indian legend be based on fact? Could the "strange looking men" have been the Culdee monks at Mystery Hill, disappearing into their bothain tunnels and chambers, after converting a tribe of Indians to Christianity? I suppose we shall never know. I, of course, shall never know either if the evidence presented here has convinced you that it was the Irish who discovered America. As for me, however, I have no doubt that there is something Old Irish in our New England.

III
WILD GEESE AND WHITE BLACKBIRDS

The ship ST. PATRICK arrived in Boston from Ireland on March 15, 1636, with wools, livestock, and "wild Irish girls" — servants for the Puritan settlers of the New World. When she sailed by Castle Island, a lieutenant from the island-fort rowed out to the ship and demanded of her Captain Palmer that he "strike the Irish flag". The captain obeyed, but he and the ST. PATRICK crew "took this as a great injury," reported Governor John Winthrop in his Journal. Captain Palmer complained to the Boston magistrates, and the haughty lieutenant was called before them to explain his action. The judges were not satisfied with his contention that the Irish flag should not wave in a New England port. They ordered him to go aboard the ST. PATRICK and raise the Irish flag himself, "and acknowledge his error, so all the ship's company might receive satisfaction."

Not only were the Irish persecuted in England during the 17th Century, but in their own homeland many were driven out by the English. In New England, Irish Catholics, by law, were "not allowed to set foot". In Rhode Island, however, thanks to Welch founder and Father of the Baptists, Roger Williams (who himself was exiled by the Pilgrims and Puritans), Irish Catholics were allowed to settle. Scotch-Irish Presbyterians who left Ireland in droves in the late 1600's could enter Puritan New England, but they were treated like second-class citizens. Most were ordered to move out of the established sea-side towns to settle in the Indian infested wilds of New Hampshire, Maine, Vermont, and Western Massachusetts. A popular Puritan saying of the time was, "An Irishman in New England is as rare as a white blackbird." Old New England town records, however, reveal that a few "white blackbirds" managed to sneak in and feather their nests here as early as 1621.

The Pilgrims, who seemingly were not as strict as the Puritans, were active in shipping Irish servants and convicts into Plimouth to help them with their labors. Irish girls especially were sold into servitude, and the kidnapping of boys and girls in Ireland by unscrupulous English sea captains was common practice. The ship TALBOT, arriving first at Puritan Salem and then at Plimouth in 1629, carried "a company of 35 servants" for the Plantation, many of them from Ireland. Their names, unlike those who arrived on the MAYFLOWER nine years earlier, were not recorded. FORTUNE, the ship that followed the MAY-FLOWER to Plimouth in 1621, carried 35 Pilgrims and "Strangers"

— one being William Conner, an Irish settler who died in 1626. Two Irishmen, Stephen Tracy and Hugh Stacey, joined the Pilgrims in 1623. Tracy settled at the Plimouth Plantation and Stacey moved on to settle in Dedham.

Thomas Morton, the jovial leader of the settlement at Mount Wollaston (called "Merry Mount"), 25 miles from Plimouth "was scorned", said Governor Bradford, "even by the meanest of servants." Yet, many of the Irish servants at Plimouth snuck off to join Morton at what is now Quincy, Massachusetts. The reason for this migration was that Morton freed all the servants at "Merry Mount" and invited all, including Pilgrims and Indians, to "feast, have strong drink and other junkets." To the popular maypole which he erected at the top of the "mount", he tacked his poems. One read:
> "Give to the Nymphe that's free from Scorne,
> No Irish stuffe nor Scotch over-worne.
> Lasses in beaver coats, come away,
> Ye shall be welcome to us night and day . . ."

Apparently Morton preferred Indian girls in "beaver coats" to the Scottish and Irish girls who had joined him from Plimouth.

In the early winter of 1626, a 40-foot vessel heading for Virginia from Ireland wrecked off Cape Cod at what is now Orleans. "Most of her passengers were Irish servants," wrote Governor Bradford in his Journal, and the good Governor took them into the Plantation. Some ran away to live with the Indians, and "one Mr. Fells and his servant girl, fled to Cape Anne and then to Boston, "after it was discovered that the Irish servant girl was his mistress. Bradford informs us most of the Irish "carried themselves very orderly all ye time they stayed. They helped plant crops and assisted in the harvest." The shipwreck victims stayed in Plimouth until the following late Summer, "when they took passage to Virginia."

Probably the most controversial Irish–Pilgrim was John Lyford. Even though he was not of their faith, he arrived in Plimouth with his family in 1624 to minister to them. The Pilgrims didn't like his teachings and, like Thomas Morton, he didn't get along with Captain "Shrimp" Standish. The Pilgrims got rid of him. He went to Gloucester to preach to Roger Conant's fisherman — but they didn't like Lyford either, so he sailed off to Virginia where he died a few years later.

The ship GOODFELLOW arrived in Puritan Boston in the Spring of 1654, with hundreds of Irish men and women who were immediately sold into servitude. Cotton Mather, the most prominent Puritan minister of the time, said that their arrival "is a formidable attempt of Satan and his sons to unsettle us." Mather was not horrified at the fact that the Irish prisoners were being sold as slaves, but that they would be rubbing shoulders with the New England gentry. It was Mather who, 34 years later, had an old Irish washer woman (Mrs. Glover) hanged as a witch on Boston Common. He charged that she "tormented her neighbor's children" and would not answer the Judge in English, "but only in Irish, which was her native tongue."

One of Cotton Mather's best friends, and one of America's first authors, was Nathaniel Ward of Ipswich, who had been excommunicated from the Anglican Church in England in 1633. His writings probably best summarize the 17th Century Puritan feelings toward the Irish. "Cursed be he," writes Ward, "that maketh not his sword starke drunk with Irish blood." Cotton Mather was the first to admit, however, that, "Ward didn't like anyone."

One of the first recorded Irish Catholics in Puritan New England was Teague Crehan of Dorchester, Massachusetts, who was here in 1640. According to Savage's Geneological Dictionary, Crehan was "stolen from his parents in Ireland as a mere child." Also settled into Dorchester a few years later, was "Peter O'Kelley, wife and family." Richard Kelley lived in Newbury, Massachusetts in the 1640's, and "John McCarthy-Irishman," lived in Boston in 1634. "Edward Nealand," with the designation "Irishman" beside his name, showed up in the Ipswich records of 1653; and John Mackshene, William Murphy, Roger Morey, Thomas Moriarity, and Clifford Byrne were all Salem seamen in the mid 1600's. Murphy became Captain of the ship FRIENDSHIP in 1670, and Teague Cantey became a Master Mariner out of Boston in 1672.

There were even a few Irishmen who worked their way into the elite pecking order of Puritan society. One was William Hibbins, who arrived in Salem from Ireland aboard the MARY AND JOHN in 1634. He married Governor Richard Bellingham's sister, became a Boston Magistrate, and died here in 1654 a comparatively wealthy man. His wife, Ann Hibbins, died two years later, hanged as a witch on Boston Common. Her property was bequeathed to her sons, John and Joseph of Ballyhorick, County Cork, Ireland.

Another Irishman who married a Governor's sister was George Downing of Dublin, who arrived in Boston at age 14, in 1638. After graduating from Harvard, he married Governor John Winthrop's sister. A few years after Governor Winthrop died, his widow Martha married

Irishman John Cogan, the first man to open a store in the Town of Boston, on March 4, 1634. Like Downing, Cogan was in the first class to graduate from Harvard College. When he died in 1658, he bequeathed 175 acres of land in Chelsea to Harvard.

The Civil War in England, and Oliver Cromwell's subsequent invasion of Ireland in the 1640's, "drove many Irish Catholics to Massachusetts," writes Scott Paradise in his "History Of Essex County." Also, the fall of Limerick, Ireland to the English in 1691 and the famous Battle of the Boyne in 1690 — further dividing Catholics and Protestants — caused a massive immigration of Catholic Irishmen to foreign lands. After the Battle of Limerick, England's William of Orange gave Irish Catholic soldiers the choice of remaining in Ireland under English rule, or joining the French and leaving their homeland forever. An English flag and a French flag were set outside the gates of Limerick, and the Irish Army marched out of the town to stand behind the flag of their choice. Only 1,048 Irish soldiers joined the English, and over 14,000 chose the French flag, and a few days later set sail for France. They and their descendants, from that day to this, have been known as "The Wild Geese". Most of these fighting Irishmen joined the French Army, others moved on to Spain, Austria, Poland, and America. Within the following fifty years, the most decorated unit in the French Army was "The Irish Brigade".

During New England's King Philip's War in 1675, thousands of Colonists were killed in skirmishes and battles with the Indians. An estimated 8% of the Colonial Army fighting King Philip and his rebellious tribes was Irish-born. After the War, New England was in a deep depression, in desparate need of food. Only one country came to New England's aid — Ireland. The Mayor of Dublin and the citizens of the Irish capitol fitted out the ship KATHERINE and loaded her with free food and clothes for the "cold, starving Americans." The KATHERINE stopped at almost every New England port, distributing goods to 47 villages and towns and saving 2,350 people from certain starvation — this made the Puritans a bit more tolerant of the Irish.

From 1691 throughout the early 18th Century, 30 to 40 ships a year sailed into New England ports carrying Irish linens, wool, livestock, salted meats, cheese, butter, and immigrants. The English did everything in their power to stop this trade between Ireland and America, and in Ulster, Northern Ireland, where many Scotch-Irish Presbyterians had settled in 1603, the English forced them out of the wool and linen trade. Then, in 1698, the English insisted that all Scotch-Irish citizens of Ireland conform to Anglican worship. Many refused, so they migrated in great numbers to Virginia, North Carolina, and New England. The Puritans, for the most part, gave them the cold shoulder and as one prominent Puritan minister announced from the pulpit; "They keep the Sabbath, and anything else they can get their hands on."

When the Irish and Scotch-Irish arrived in New England, they were ordered to push on into the wilderness, and were not allowed to remain in any seaside town for more than a week or two. The Puritans had decided to use them as a buffer against Indian attacks on the established Puritan villages and towns. In this manner, some 500 new villages were established in New England, all founded and settled by the Irish and Scotch-Irish. Some settlements, like Worcester, Massachusetts, grew into large cities, whereas others, like Londonderry, Derry, and Dublin, New Hampshire, remain small towns. At Kennebec, Maine a large Irish settlement named "Cork" was eliminated when attacked by Indians in 1726. The few Irish survivors of this massacre, either moved into New Hampshire or moved on to Pennsylvania.

The ships from Ireland kept streaming into New England ports throughout the early 1700's with products to trade and people to transport into the wilderness. In one day alone, August 4, 1718, five ships arrived in Boston from Ireland with a total of 1,560 Irish immigrants. One of the ships was the MAYFLOWER from Ballyshannon, not the Pilgrim MAYFLOWER, but another ship of the same name. "CHARMING MOLLY, Captain James Finney — 162 passengers from Ireland; SALLY from Kinsgate, Ireland - 59 days passage, with many passengers from Ireland; Brigantine BOOTLE, nineteen transports and other passengers from Ireland," these are typical of Boston Port traffic records, dated 1736. Captain Philip Bass came before the Boston Selectmen on September 24, 1724, to report that his ship in the harbor "has an infectious sickness of my Irish passengers." They all had the measles, including Captain Bass. He was ordered to take them and himself to Spectacle Island in the outer harbor, "til they be cured."

Many of the new Irish didn't want to go out into the woods to face the Indians, and they preferred to stay in the seacoast towns. "Great numbers of persons have very lately bin transported from Ireland into this Province, and because of Indian Troubles, resided in this Towne," - Boston Towne Records, May 3, 1723. In the Boston Towne Records dated June 13, 1719, we get the Puritan fathers' message loud and clear: "John Macinnis, wife and four children, John Henderson, wife and five children, Francis Gray, wife and three children, John Criton and one maid: All arriving from Ireland two months ago, are warned to depart this Towne." The Boston Magistrates, in 1723, warned Massachusetts Lt. Governor John Wentworth — then acting as Governor of New Hampshire, that "because of the many Irish settling into the Merrimack Valley, you should take precautions for their safety against Indians."

Poet John Greenleaf Whittier, himself a product of the Merrimack Valley, wrote "that of the Irish who settled here about the year 1720, they brought indeed with them, among other strange matters, potatoes and fairies." Although an attempt was made to establish the potato in Virginia in 1573, it was first successfully domesticated in Ireland, and from there was introduced into New England by the Irish settlers. Londonderry, New Hampshire claims to be the first place that a potato was grown in America, and in Maine, potatoes are still a major crop. "The potato and the farmer took root and flourished among us," Whittier continues, "but the fairies died out, after lingering a few years in a very melancholy and disconsolate way, looking regretfully back to their green turf dances, moonlight revels, and cheerful nestling around the shealing fires of Ireland."

With the leprechauns, or "Irish fairies" as Whittier called them, came the spinning-wheel and skillful Irish weavers. Beginning in 1721, and continuing throughout that century, except when the British occupied Boston, there was a public spinning contest and exhibition on Boston Common every August 8th. "All classes of Irish met and vied with each other in skill," a Boston diarist wrote in 1740, "with a great concourse of people from Town and Country." Thousands turned out to watch the Irish colleens spin, stomping their feet to the fiddle, and listening to the Irish men, who could spin a yarn or two themselves. The Irish weavers were there too, working looms from large portable stages set up on the Common. New England historians, including the prominent Samuel Adams Drake, estimate that from 50% to 90% of all clothes worn by Americans in the mid 1700's, were made by the Irish.

The Society of Linen Manufacturers was established by Irishmen in Massachusetts, in 1749. The man who established the manufacture of finished cloth items in America, building a number of mills in Waltham, Lowell, and other New England towns, was Patrick Tracy Jackson, of Newburyport, Massachusetts, whose parents came from Ireland. His brother James, was co-founder with Dr. Joseph Warren, of Boston's famous Mass. General Hospital, and he was the hospital's first physician. A third brother, Charles Jackson, was a Superior Court Judge.

In Rhode Island in 1728, lived the daughter of an Irish Chief Justice, who refused to wear anything but "Irish homespun." She was the wife of famous philosopher, George Berkeley, who became the Anglican Bishop of Cloyne in Dublin in 1734. While living at Newport, Berkeley wrote "The Minute Philosopher," but more important to him, he met and befriended an Irish missionary to the Indians, Dr. James McSparran. McSparran not only helped and taught the Indians, but he studied the medicines of their witch-doctors. When Berkeley called the Indians "savages", McSparran corrected him, saying that, "it isn't the Narragansetts who are savages, but the ruling English who are savages." When Berkeley returned to Ireland a few years later, he wrote, "The Querist," in which he asks his many English readers and followers, "What do you intend to do about the poverty, sickness and distress of poor Ireland? Whose fault is it if poor Ireland still continues poor?" As Bishop of Cloyne, he represented 1,000 Anglican Irish and 10,000 Irish Catholics, and he became political and patriotic leader for all of them. The English didn't like his probing questions, yet his books were more popular in England than those of any other writer of his time.

When a lingering frost ruined Ireland's potato crops, causing a nation wide famine from 1739 through 1741, forcing another great exodus from Ireland to America, Berkeley personally saved an estimated 10,000 lives. Using a dysentery cure he obtained from McSparran, who had learned about it from the Rhode Island Indians, Berkeley treated the sick Irish. It was a New England pine tar solution, called "tar-water". During this 18th Century famine, Berkeley and his wife turned their Dublin home into a dispensary, saving thousands from certain death. His life long dream had been to be savior of the American Indians, but instead, he became savior of the poor and destitute Irish. As noted Irish author, Jonathan Swift wrote, "if we Anglican-Irish had Saints like the Catholic Irish, George Berkeley would be one."

Two of Jonathan Swift's next door Dublin neighbors, Anthony and Lemuel Gulliver, emigrated to New England in the early 1700's, settling in Milton, Massachusetts. Anthony remained in Milton, but Lemuel was not happy in America, and he longed to return to Ireland. One day in 1723, on the road to Boston, Irish born James Boies of Dorchester, found Lemuel sitting along the roadside, crying his eyes out. He was running away from his Milton home, going to Boston to hop a ship back to Ireland, but he had no money for the passage. Boies, who was comparatively wealthy from founding some new businesses in the Boston area, took Lemuel to Boston and paid his way back home to Dublin. "I did so, for the lad was in agony," Boies later reported to Anthony Glover. Upon arriving home, Lemuel delighted in telling his friends and neighbors, including Jonathan Swift, embellished tales about life in

New England. "The frogs in the bogs about Boston are as tall as my knees," he said, "and they have musical voices like guitars. The mosquitos have bills as long as darning needles," he reported. Lemuel Gulliver's exaggerated stories prompted Jonathan Swift to write a novel, published in 1726, and titled "Gulliver's Travels," one of the great classics of world literature.

James Boies, the man who sent Gulliver back to his homeland, is noted for starting America's first chocolate factory with his fellow Irishman, John Hanon, in 1765, at Dorchester. Six years later he and his son-in-law, Irishman Hugh McLean, founded New England's first successful paper mill, also in Dorchester, Massachusetts. John Hanon, however, like Lemuel Gulliver, decided to return to Ireland. He left Boston on Saint Patrick's Day, 1776, on the ship MINERVA — Captain Callahan commanding. It was the last vessel to leave Boston Harbor that day, as the British evacuated the town. John Hanon didn't leave because he was lonely for his homeland — he was a Tory.

On Saint Patrick's Day, 1737, "The Charitable Irish Society", the first Irish organization formed in America, held its first meeting in Boston — there were 26 members present, "all of Irish blood." Their primary mission was to bring more destitute Irish families to New England and to help poor Irish folks who were already here. Most were sea captains, some were merchants. One was Peter Pelham, known today as New England's "Father of Fine Arts", for he started an engraving and art school in Boston in 1737. Later, he married Richard Copley's widow, who was the daughter of an Irish Squire. Her son (one of Pelham's art students) was the famous portrait painter, John Singleton Copley. One member, who later became President of the Irish Society, was William Mackay. With the American Revolution looming, and Boston being the hub of British-American turmoil, he stood before his Irish and Irish-American colleagues and said: "We shall conquer one of the greatest and most potent nations on the globe. May our friends and countrymen in Ireland behave like all brave Americans, so that they too may recover their liberties."

Most Americans today, including those of Irish blood, believe that the Irish came to America during the potato famine of the mid 1800's. Indeed, many did come then, but thousands immigrated in the 17th and 18th Centuries. By the time of the American Revolution, the Wild Geese and White Blackbirds who had flocked to New England were quite nestled in. Claws sharpened, they were more than ready to spread their wings with the American eagle, and become birds of prey.

IV
THE IRISH MASSACRE

The Irish were taking over Boston in 1770, or so thought the proper Bostonians. Most were dock workers, fishermen, and laborers, constantly drinking and fighting in dock-side pubs, and accused of "rowdyism" by the Boston gentry. They were called "Teagues" and "Paddies" by New Englanders, for many of their first names were Teague or Padrig. Some of these "Bogtrotters", as they were also called, were Scotch-Irish Presbyterians, but most were Irish Catholics, who had been filtering into the port from Ireland for over 25 years. "It is suggested that there are several Roman Catholics that now dwell and reside in this Towne," the Boston Records of September 22, 1746, reveal, "and it may be very dangerous to permit such persons to reside here, in case we should be attacked by the enemy." The "enemy" that the Boston town fathers feared in 1746 was Catholic French Canada, bordering New England in the North; but in 1770, Bostonians were aware of a new "enemy" in their midst.

Over 2,000 British soldiers roamed the streets of Boston, half of them Irishmen who had been recruited by the British in Dublin. They were housed at Murray Barracks near the Custom House in downtown Boston, and had occupied the town for a year and a half. Residents and shop owners snubbed and insulted them; they, in turn, harrassed the citizens to the point where an all-out conflict seemed inevitable. The spark that ignited the initial conflict, occured on Friday afternoon, March 2nd, 1770.

Private Matthew Kilroy of the 29th British Regiment, a tough Dubliner with a quick temper, who had been accused a few weeks earlier of theft, went looking for off-duty part time work along the Boston waterfront. Approaching Samuel Gray's Ropewalk, he asked the owner to hire him as a ropemaker. "You want work do ye?" asked Gray, mimicking Kilroy's Irish brogue. "Aye!!" replied the Redcoat. "Well then," said Gray, winking at the other ropemakers who had gathered around him, "ye may start by cleaning my shithouse." The others roared with delight, but Kilroy didn't think it was funny. He punched Gray in the nose. The workers then pounced on Kilroy, giving him a good beating and driving him from the ropewalk. Before nightfall, Kilroy was back at the ropewalk with twelve of his Dublin pals from Murray Barracks. A real donnybrook broke out between Redcoats and ropemakers, resulting in many cracked skulls and broken noses, but the ropemakers were victorious. The soldiers retreated back to the barracks to lick their wounds. That night, a threat filtered through the British regiments and was repeated to Boston residents: "Those Bostonians as would eat their suppers on Monday night, would never eat another!" Over the weekend, Sam Adams, leader of the "Liberty Boys", a secret society of mechanics, craftsmen, and laborers bent on ridding Boston of Redcoats, decided that the ropemakers would need his help on Monday night. All members of this secret and active patriotic society, considered by many Bostonians to be "a mob of toughs", disguised themselves and used aliases when out on the streets of Boston about their business. The mob leader was "Joyce Junior," an alias with an Irish ring to it, probably chosen from an Irish masked man named Joyce, Jr. who allegedly executed King Charles I of England. Abigail Adams, wife of John Adams, Sam's cousin, informed him that, "Joyce Junior, (mounted on horseback, with a red coat, a white wig, and a drawn sword), escorted by a band of nearly 500, carted five Tory villains to Boston town limits and warned them never to return." Who was this mysterious Joyce Junior? Some thought he was Sam Adams, but even to this day, no one knows for sure just whom he was. Certainly, Sam Adams made a careful plan, preparing to meet Kilroy's threat of revenge on the evening of Monday, March 5 th.

It was a cold night, streets glazed with ice, and a light snow falling. At about 7:30 p.m., a group of over 200 ropemakers, dock workers, shop owners, fishermen, and laborers, gathered at Dock Square near Boston's Faneuil Hall. A tall man, wearing a white wig and red coat, spoke to them for some twenty minutes. He seemed to work them into a frenzy, for after his speech they marched off shouting and singing, every one of them, but the man in the red coat. He slipped away as the others started up the hill towards King Street and the British Custom House. Nobody knows who the disguised man in the red coat was, or what he said. Most historians believe that the mysterious man who whipped up the Faneuil Hall crowd was Irishman William Molyneux, one of the leaders of the "Liberty Boys."

Molyneux was from Dublin, where he had been a physician, active in the cause for Ireland's freedom. He had written the patriotic book "Case of Ireland", of which Ben Franklin said, "in it, our part is warmly taken by the Irish". Lecky, the British historian, wrote, "the treatise of Molyneux in defense of Irish liberty, was the text-book of American freedom." Molyneux lived on Boston's Beacon Street, across from the Common, and his next door neighbor was John Hancock. He was known for his patriotic zeal and for his oratory. A poem by him can be seen to this day, scratched into a window pane with his diamond ring at Sudbury's Wayside Inn. It reads: "What do you think. Here is good drink. Perhaps you may not know it. If not in haste, do stop and taste, And you merry folk will shew it." This poetic etching on the window is signed and dated, "June 24, 1774 - Boston." William Molyneux died a few months later of a heart attack, when British troops were camped on Boston Common across from his home.

Whether or not the speech on Dock Square was delivered by William Molyneux and inspired by Sam Adams, we'll never know, but it set a crowd into action. As they marched noisily into the downtown area, the bell of the North End Church began ringing loudly — the signal to the people of Boston that there was a fire in progress — though there was no fire in Boston that evening. Hearing the bell, people ran out into the streets from their homes and shops, most of them carrying fire buckets. Many of them joined the marchers heading up the hill, singing, yelling, and laughing as they proceeded.

At approximately the same time, four young Bostonians on nearby Brattle Street took a short cut down Boylston Alley. They later reported that, "in the alley we met a British sentry armed with a cutlass, and with him was a mean looking Irishman who carried a stout cudgel." The British sentry and the Irishman made aggressive movements towards them, they said. According to the British sentry, who was interviewed later, "two of them would not answer my challenges to stop and be identified." An argument and then a fight broke out, during which one of the Americans was cut on the arm by the sentry's cutlass, and he was hit with a club. The "mean-looking Irishman," probably an off-duty Dublin Redcoat, hit two of the young men with his cudgel, then ran to the British barracks for help. British soldiers, carrying shovels and fire-tongs, crowded into the alley and severely beat up one of the young men. The other three ran off and met up with part of the boisterous crowd coming up from Dock Square. They rushed into the alley, swinging fists and sticks. The soldiers quickly retreated back to Murray Barracks. Then, twelve Redcoats armed with bayonets emerged from the barracks looking for a fight, but by this time the crowd in the alley had dispersed. "Where are the Yankee boogers?" one of the fleeing boys heard an Irish Redcoat yell. The soldiers, intent on finding the trouble-makers, trotted off toward Dock Square.

When the detail of Redcoats tried to return to their barracks, they were met by some 100 Bostonians, who surrounded them and pelted them with snowballs. One soldier aimed his musket at the crowd, but at that moment a British officer came out of the messhall and knocked the musket from his hands, then ordered all soldiers back into the barracks.

About the same time, on Brattle Street, a British Captain named Goldsmith walked out of Piemont's Barbershop without paying for his haircut and shave. The barber's apprentice, a boy of 13, followed the Captain down the street shouting at him to pay his bill. When the pair entered King Street — the boy following and cursing Goldsmith from a few paces behind him — the Redcoat on duty in front of the Custom House stepped from his sentry box and told the boy to stop bothering the Captain. Goldsmith walked on as the sentry, Pvt. Hugh Montgomery, attempted to stop the boy from following. The boy dodged around the sentry, calling him many names unfit to print. Montgomery chased him and cuffed him on the side of the head with his musket. "I'm killed!" shouted the boy and he ran off crying, just in time to meet the large crowd of ropemakers, laborers, and dock workers, who were approaching the Custom House. Montgomery ducked back into his sentry box, as some 200 angry Bostonians started pelting him with snowballs, iceballs, sticks, and stones.

Leading the mob, "was a tall mulatto fellow," Crispus Attucks, a laborer at the Boston fruit market. He was half black and half American Indian. 'He had two clubs in his hands," said Patrick Keaton, a recent immigrant from Ireland, who was with Attucks. "Here, take one of them," said Attucks, handing Keaton one of his clubs, "and so, I had me a weapon," Keaton later testified, "thanks to that big black fella." The crowd pushed in on Private Montgomery, who cowered in his little sentry box outside the Custom House. He nervously loaded his musket and began shouting loudly for help. He then aimed his musket at Crispus Attucks, who was closest to him, screeching above the curses of the crowd to, "call out the guard!"

"If you fire, you'll swing for it," Henry Knox, a Scotch-Irish bookseller from Belfast, Ireland shouted at Montgomery, as he stepped in front of Attucks. "I'll blow their bloody brains out," replied the trembling sentry. The words were but out of his mouth, when British officer-of-the-day Thomas Preston, a Scotch-Irishman, came trotting up the street from Murray Barracks with seven armed Redcoats in single file. The Redcoats were; James Hategan, William Wemms, John Carroll, William Warren, William McCauley, Hugh White, and Matthew Kilroy; five of them were Irishmen from Dublin. Loading their muskets and attaching bayonets, they took up a line beside Private Montgomery. "Do you mean to fire on these people?" Knox shouted at Preston over the cat-calls and curses of the crowd. "By no means," Preston replied, as he and his men were pelted with snowballs, some with cutting oyster and clam shells packed into them. As

Montgomery left the sentry box to join his fellow soldiers, he lowered his musket and Attucks, seizing the opportunity, knocked the musket from his hands and wrestled Montgomery to the ground. The mob closed in on the other Redcoats, some of them shouting, "Kill them! Kill the bloody lobster-backs!"

"Present your arms!" Preston ordered, and the Redcoats aimed their muskets. For a brief moment their was silence in the pressing crowd, then someone from the British ranks shouted "Fire!". To this day, no one knows who gave this devastating command, but it wasn't Captain Preston. It was probably Private Kilroy who gave the order, for he had spotted Samuel Gray — owner of the ropewalk — in the crowd, and his first musket ball went into Gray's head. Gray fell back dead. Montgomery, who by this time had retrieved his musket, shot Crispus Attucks, as did Private William Warren, both musket balls exploding into his chest. Sailor James Caldwell had apparently started to run away — as did most of the crowd — when the Redcoats opened fire. He dropped to the snow covered street with two holes in his back. Another musketball ripped through 17 year old laborer Sam Maverick, and Patrick Carr — a recent immigrant from Ireland — was shot in the stomach. The Redcoats relaoded, and six more Bostonians fell as they fired again. The Redcoats stood their ground as the crowd retreated in panic, running off in every direction. Captain Preston was shocked at the scene before him, but Private Kilroy was pleased. He stepped forward to finalize his predicted night of violence by thrusting his bayonet into the lifeless body of Samuel Gray.

Three were killed outright, two were mortally wounded, and six recovered from their wounds. Boston was up in arms and wanted British blood, a goal Sam Adams had been striving for, for years. His mission of getting Redcoats out of Boston was accomplished overnight. The Royal Governor removed all British soldiers from the town to Castle Island. Captain Preston and the eight Boston Massacre privates, went to jail to await trial. Sam Adams wrote scathing articles in the local newspapers about the Massacre and Paul Revere made engravings for the newspapers and for posters. He depicted British troops firing on the defenseless people, calling the Custom House in his engravings "Butchers Hall."

It took Irishman Patrick Carr nine days to die from his belly wound. "An agonizing torture," said Sam Adams, but Sam changed his mind about, "that brave Irishman," when he learned that of the 96 eyewitnesses who testified that the Redcoats had fired without provocation, only one said that they fired in self-defense — Patrick Carr. "In Ireland," said Carr from his death bed, "I have seen mobs that soldiers would not bear half so much, before they fired." His final words were, "I hold no malice toward any man." Sam Adams was furious at Carr. He told his cousin John Adams that, "the poor immigrant is a Catholic, and, of course, his words mean nothing." John Adams, who became second President of the United States 26 years later, thought differently. At the pleading of one of Captain Preston's American friend, James Forester — a Scotch-Irishman nicknamed, "The Irish Infant" — John Adams agreed to defend the British soldiers in court — a job that no other lawyer in New England would take. His only hope of saving Preston and his men from the gallows, was Carr's sworn testimony. Preston's trial was held in Boston on October 24, 1770, and Adams was successful in having the jury made up of New Englanders come to a verdict of "not guilty."

The trial of the eight Redcoat privates followed on November 20, 1770. John Adams claimed that the soldiers fired in self defense at "a motley mob of saucy boys, negroes, mulattoes, Irish Teagues, and outlandish Jacktars." John's friends, and even his own father, thought his statement was disgraceful. His adversary during the trial was Robert Treat Paine, who was adamant in his plea that the Redcoats were guilty of murder. According to O'Hart, in his "History Of Ireland", Paine's grandfather and great-uncle, Robert and Henry O'Neill, were from Dungannon Ireland, and in order to save their land and estate from being confiscated by the English after the Battle of Limerick, they adopted their mother's maiden name of Paine.

After Adams' and Paine's verbal battles in the courthouse, the New England jury, made up of "out-of-towners," found six of the Redcoats "not guilty". Private Montgomery and Kilroy were found not guilty of murder, but guilty of manslaughter. Judge Mayo decided not to send them to jail, but have them each branded on the thumb with a red-hot poker. They screeched and cursed as the letter "M" was scorched into their skin, then they were released into continued service with the British Army. Bostonians and most New Englanders were not satisfied with the light punishment, and the winds of war began to stir, constantly fanned by Sam Adams. A Dublin rabble-rouser had stuck his nose into Sam's business, and unknowingly became his pawn for rebellion. The "Father of the American Revolution," although outwardly outraged that the so-called instigator of the Boston Massacre, Matthew Kilroy, had escaped with no more than a sore thumb, inwardly he must have been delighted that "Kilroy was here".

V
IRISH PIRATES

The newly built sloop SQUIRREL sailed down the Annisquam River and headed out to sea on a routine few days of fishing. At the helm was Irishman Andrew Haraden. In his coarse brogue he issued orders to his five Gloucester crew members to prepare the lines. Furthest from his mind was the possibility that his little craft would be attacked by pirates, but waiting for him outside Gloucester Harbor was the notorious buccaneer John Philip and his cut-throat crew. Pirate John Philip had captured 34 New England vessels within the previous year of 1723, and had mercilessly tortured or killed their captains and crews. Philip, in his larger armed ship with a crew ten times the size of Haraden's, easily overtook the SQUIRREL. Before attempting to do away with the fishermen, the pirates decided to put them to work refitting their sloop as an armed flagship for Philip. This gave Haraden enough time to persuade some of the pirate crew to mutiny against their leader. At a given signal from Haraden, fisherman Ed Cheesman seized the pirate who was second in command, John Nott, and threw him overboard. Haraden then picked up a nearby boarding axe and lobbed off the heads of pirate chief John Philip and that of another pirate named Burrell. All the pirates who didn't agree to help the fishermen were either killed or followed John Nott into the Atlantic. The SQUIRREL then sailed back to the Annisquam River with John Philip's head hanging from the masthead. That evening, May 1, 1724, Irish Andy Haraden was cheered through the streets of Gloucester. One of the pirates whom Haraden managed to rehabilitate and who aided him in taking over the pirate ship was John Fillmore, whose great-grandson became the thirteenth President of the United States. Andy Haraden's grandson, however, became a pirate - or at least that's what the British called him; to the Americans, he was the most patriotic pirate who ever lived.

"They are Rebels and Pirates, and we promise the gallows to those taken prisoner," was the decree of British Parliament concerning American privateersmen in 1775. Neither the stigma of "pirate" nor the threat of execution deterred the sea-rovers of New England from taking on the British Navy, the mightest maritime force in the World. America had no warships at all, and her commercial ports were all but destitute of any vessels that carried cannons. At the outset of the Revolution, Boston and New York Harbors were held by the British, then Newport, Rhode Island and other major seaports up and down the Atlantic coast were closed to the Rebels. The only active dens for privateering activity in Massachusetts, were Salem, Marblehead,

Beverly, Gloucester, and Newburyport. Portsmouth, New Hampshire and Connecticut ports were open as well, but were continuously guarded by British warships that cruised outside the harbors; yet, from these ports, American commerce survived, military supplies to the Colonial Army were provided, and Britania who ruled the waves, was challenged and finally defeated.

There were many brave and daring New England privateersmen, but the most heroic and successful of the lot were the Tracy and O'Brien brothers of Newburyport, Hugh Hill of Beverly, and Simon Forrester and Jonathan Haraden of Salem — All were either Irish born or of Irish descent.

The first act of Colonial piracy did not occur off the shores of Massachusetts, however, but at Machias, Maine, on June 12, 1775. The British cutter MARGARETTA arrived in that port for lumber to build barracks for the British troops in Boston. She was attacked in the bay by an American sloop loaded with Minutemen and led by Jeremiah O'Brien, a relative of the Newburyport O'Briens. In hand-to-hand combat, the Machias Minutemen captured the cutter and another sloop that was escorting her. Three of the British sailors were killed, including the MARGARETTA's captain, and six were wounded. The other British sailors were taken captive and marched to Massachusetts. Two Maine Minutemen were killed in the battle and five were wounded. Besides the vessels, the booty they collected was, "four double fortified three pounder cannons, fourteen swivel guns, and a number of small arms." Although O'Brien and his men continued to cruise the Maine coast, capturing or destroying as many British vessels as they could find, it wasn't until August 23, 1775, that the Massachusetts Provincial Congress legalized his piracy: "Jeremiah O'Brien, is hereby commissioned as Commander of the armed schooner DILIGENT and the sloop MACHIAS LIBERTY, for the purpose of guarding the sea coast, for the sum of one hundred and sixty pounds lawful money of this Colony of supplying the men with provisions and ammunition..." Thus, Jeremiah O'Brien became America's first official privateersman. To this day, this has meant to the people of Maine that Machias was the Birthplace of the American Navy - a claim that is hotly contested in Beverly and Marblehead, Massachusetts.

The distinction between pirate and privateersman was a thin one, but there was a distinction, even though the British continued to call American privateersmen "pirates" throughout the Revolution. A pirate was a seagoing outlaw with allegiance to no country, and at war with everyone; whereas a privateersman was a plundering warrior of the sea recognized by, and often commissioned by, a local government or country.

The first privateer commissioned by General George Washington, Commander of America's armed forces, was the schooner HANNAH out of Beverly. She was owned by General John Glover, and commanded and manned by Marbleheaders. Washington's orders to Captain Nicholson Broughton, dated September 5, 1775, were: "take command... and proceed on board the schooner HANNAH at Beverly, lately fitted out and equipped with arms and ammunition and provisions at the Continental expence..." That same day, the HANNAH was chased into Gloucester Harbor by the 20-gun HMS LIVELY, and seven days later the Marblehead crew mutinied because they didn't get a share of prize money from a vessel they had captured - a vessel which Washington said was American and not British.

Most of the thousands of New England men and boys who sailed in privateers, preferred joining the crews of those owned and operated by local merchants than those sponsored by Washington and the government. The reason being that Congress only allowed one-third of the value of a captured vessel and cargo to be divided among the captain and crew, whereas most privately owned privateers offered half the value of a captured prize to the captain and crew. Of course, these privateering ventures by local merchants weren't always profitable, and sometimes were financially devastating. John and Patrick Tracy of Newburyport, for example, lost 41 ships before the Revolution was two years old.

At the opposite extreme, there was Irish born Hugh Hill commanding the privateer CICERO out of Beverly, who captured several wealthy prizes, including the British ship MERCURY off Spain that was carrying 15,000 pounds in gold. Hill later sailed out of Beverly with 140 men in the newly built privateer, PILGRIM. On September 2, 1778, he headed her for the British Isles. Within six weeks, in quick succession, the PILGRIM battled and captured; the 200-ton PAULA, the ship ANDREW, brig WILLIAM, schooner CHARMING SALLY, brig BROTHERS, ship ANNA ELIZA, bark SUCCESS, and the brigantine HOPE. The commander of the HOPE was Captain Graves, whom Hill recognized as a British officer who whipped him many years before when he was serving as a cabin boy. Hugh had Graves stripped to the waist and tied to the mast, then repayed an old debt.

The PILGRIM, touting a mere 16 guns and taking ships twice her size with many more cannons, returned from her maiden voyage on

January 13, 1779, to Beverly where there was a great celebration that night. The crew had but time to catch their breath when Hugh Hill was heading the PILGRIM back out toward his old homeland again. Off the coast of Ireland, he captured many British ships. The PILGRIM held so many prisoners that Hill was forced to drop them all off on land — but he chose the remotest section of Western Ireland to do so. On February 9, 1781, he was back in Beverly with the British ship MARS in tow. Hill had captured her in the Irish Channel after a bloody battle. Part of her cargo was a collection of rare books, owned by distinguished Irish scientist Dr. Richard Kirwan of Dublin. Beverly and Salem merchants wrote to Kirwan, offering to pay for the books, but Kirwan refused payment, saying that he hoped the Americans "will make good use of them." The Kirwin books inspired the creation of the Salem Athenaeum, once considered the finest library in America, and still in operation on Essex Street, across from the Salem Public Library.

Simon Forrester of Cork, Ireland, like Hugh Hill, joined the crew of a ship sailing to America when he was a youth, and then settled in Salem, Massachusetts. During the Revolution he commanded the privateers; ROVER, JASON, PATTY, and PORT PACKET and later became a wealthy Salem merchant. The 158 privateers that sailed out of Salem during the Revolution captured 445 British prizes, and Forrester was the second most successful privateersman in bringing in booty to that port, but first prize went to Jonathan Haraden.

Jonathan Haraden, Irish Andy's grandson, born in Gloucester, and brought up in Salem, was the most daring and successful privateersman who ever lived. As a high-seas warrior, John Barry, Irish born "Father of the American Navy," can not compare, nor can Scots born John Paul Jones, nor Newburyport's John O'Brian in his great ship HIBERNIA, who is famous for capturing six British ships within three weeks during the War of 1812. By the time the Revolutionary War had ended, Haraden had battled and captured 62 enemy ships, carrying over 1,000 cannons, and had taken almost 3,000 British prisoners. Said Robert Cowan, an officer who sailed under him, "Haraden fought with a determination that seemed superhuman."

When the war broke out, Jon Haraden signed on as a lieutenant aboard the TYRANNICIDE, under Captain Fisk, the first ship sent to sea by the Massachusetts Provincial Congress, and also claimed by some to be the first ship of the American Navy. Because of his spunk and seamanship abilities, Haraden was soon commander of the TYRANNICIDE. Like Hugh Hill, he liked to harrass shipping around the British Isles, hitting the enemy closer to home. He captured many prizes there, including the heavily armed British frigate REVENGE. After almost two years on the TYRANNICIDE, he became commander of the 14-gun, 45-man GENERAL PICKERING and later the JULIUS CAESAR, both privateers out of Salem.

Haraden always seemed to pick a fight with vessels that were bigger than his, had larger crews, and carried more cannons. Such was the case while cruising off the Bay of Biscay in the PICKERING in April 1780. He pulled his privateer along side a 22-gun, 70-man British schooner, the GOLDEN EAGLE in the dead of night, and ordered the British commander to, "strike your colors or I'll sink you with a broadside!" To Harraden's surprise the commander obeyed and surrendered his ship. Harraden took most of the prisoners aboard the PICKERING, and placed some of his crew aboard the GOLDEN EAGLE. Next day, however, the 40-gun, 150-man British privateer ARCHILLES attacked and recaptured the GOLDEN EAGLE, and then prepared to battle the PICKERING. The three hour fight took place close to shore, with over 100,000 Spaniards on the cliffs and in little boats cheering on the Americans. "The PICKERING looked like a long boat beside the great ship ARCHILLES," reported eye-witness Robert Cowan, "yet Haraden was all the while calm and steady, where the shot flew around him in the thousands, as amidst a shower of snowflakes." The towering British ship could not wrack the PICKERING with an effective broadside because she sat so low in the water, and Haraden thanked a heavy cargo of sugar he had put aboard for that. He just continued peppering the ARCHILLES hull until she heeled, with tattered rigging, and finally limped away. He then recaptured the GOLDEN EAGLE. That evening, the Spaniards celebrated him by parading him through the streets on their shoulders.

On a subsequent cruise off the West Indies in the PICKERING, he battled for four hours with a 20-gun British brig twice the privateer's size, carrying eighty sailors. With only enough powder left for one more broadside, he sailed in close to the brig and shouted to her captain, "I'll give you five seconds to haul down your colors, or I'll sink you." At this point, the PICKERING was on the verge of sinking. "One . . . two . . . three . . . four," Haraden counted slowly aloud and then laughed heartily as the British hauled down their flag and surrendered.

Since word got around in the British Navy to avoid the fighting Captain Haraden, he decided to disguise his privateer into a defenseless merchantman. Sailing the Atlantic in waters frequented by two troublesome men-of-war, they approached the seemingly unarmed merchantman and headed in for the kill. Haraden's men quickly pulled off the camouflage canvas, exposing 14 cannons, and he gave both enemy ships an effective broadside — they surrendered without further fighting.

Jonathan Haraden was a daring sea rover, and a hero among heroes, but just the grandson of a fisherman, who had come to New England from Ireland to fish. If pirates hadn't interrupted his fishing, Haraden's fighting Irish spirit might never have been unleashed. He, like America herself, took on any big bully who came along, and always managed to win. As Jonathan Haraden once commented to his privateering crew, "the British always seem to bring out the best in the Irish."

Irish born privateersman Hugh Hill of Beverly, and foremost Revolutionary War privateersman, Irish-American Jon Haraden of Salem. Photos of paintings, courtesy of the Essex Institute and the Peabody Museum, Salem, MA.

Indentured Irish servant in America, Patrick Lyon the blacksmith. Painting by John Neagle, courtesy of the Boston Museum of Fine Arts.

Remains of the SPARROWHAWK that carried Irish servants to Plimouth in 1626 and shipwrecked at Orleans. Ship was salvaged from the sand and placed on display at Boston Common in 1865. Photo courtesy of the Peabody Museum, Salem, MA.

VI

REBELS AND REDCOATS

If, as the English jokingly commented in the 1600's, "the Irish in New England are as rare as white blackbirds," they were as plentiful as pigeons on Boston Common during the American Revolution. George Curtis, General George Washington's stepson, said: "that of the operations of the War, up to the coming of the French, Ireland furnished in the ratio of one hundred for one of any other nation."

"Upwards of 46,000 volunteers have been raised in Ireland," John Adams informed John Hancock on April 25, 1780. Hancock, President of the Continental Congress, was himself Scotch-Irish, his ancestors emigrating from County Down in the late 1600's. "Over 25,000 men left Ireland to fight in the American Revolution," wrote noted historian Marmion, "arriving there at a critical moment to join Washington's Army."

Early in the War, the British House of Commons was informed by Tory Joseph Galloway — who was twelve years Speaker of the Pennsylvania House, that "the greatest part of the American Army is scarcely one-fourth natives of America, about one-half Irish, and the other fourth, English and Scotch." Historian Michael J. O'Brien, who spent much of his life compiling muster roles of the Revolutionary War, concluded that 38% of Washington's Army was Irish born or of Irish descent. From Massachusetts alone, there were 3,000 Irish in America's rag-tag army.

Of the French Army that came to Newport, Rhode Island to assist General Washington, an estimated 18% were Irish — descendants of the Wild Geese. The French-Irish regiments of Colonel Dillon and Colonel Walch, demanded of General Lafayette that they be of the first in the French Army to strike the British lines.

The British also recruited Irishmen into their ranks. At the outset of the American Revolution, England's Lord Trawley announced that, "to constitute an ideal army, a general should take ten thousand fasting Scotchmen, ten thousand Englishmen after a good dinner, and the same number of Irishmen, who have just swallowed their second bottle."

Based on the frightening rumor in England that the Irish were leaving en-mass to join the American cause, British newspapers headlined, on September 21, 1775, "Irish Training To Fight Rebels". The article said that, "A Brigade of Irish Roman Catholics is forming at Munster and Connaught in order to be sent to Boston to act against the rebels . . ." The problem was that once the British trained Irishmen had shipped off to America, many of them deserted the British Army to join Washington. As early as December 17, 1774, Irishmen in the British Army were deserting. Lieutenant John Barker, who was stationed in Boston with two Irish Regiments, writes in his diary, "desertions are still too frequent among us." Six days later he wrote; "I heard of robberies committed in the Country, most probably by some of the deserters . . . Serves the Yanks right for enticing them away."

England's Lord Rawdon, who grew up in Ireland and commanded the Irish Dragoons at the Battle Of Bunker Hill, offered "ten guineas for the head of any Irish deserter," but only "five guineas if he is captured alive." In Dublin, two regiments of the British trained Irish soldiers rioted in the streets, fighting other Redcoats and their commanders, refusing to come to Boston to fight the Americans. Arthur Lee wrote to General Washington from England: "the resources of England are almost annihilated in Germany, and their last resource is the Roman Catholics of Ireland, and they have already experienced their unwillingness to fight the Americans."

At the first official battle between Redcoats and Rebels — Lexington and Concord, April 19, 1775 — 147 of the Minutemen were Irish born or Irish-Americans. Commanding the Minutemen at Concord Bridge was Colonel James Barett, son of an Irish emigrant, and the First-Sergeant in the battle was Hugh Cargil, who had arrived in New England less than a year before from Ballyshannon, Ireland.

At the Battle Of Bunker Hill (June 17,1775), in Charlestown, Massachusetts, 276 of the New England militiamen were born in Ireland. The greatest hero of the day, if indeed one man can be singled out as "the" hero, was Colonel John Stark, one of New Hampshire's regimental commanders, whose parents had emigrated to New England from County Cork in 1720. He spoke with a thick Irish brogue, and was well known in New Hampshire and Vermont as a fearless Indian fighter. Stark, with 1,200 other New Hampshire frontiersmen, mostly Irish and Scotch-Irish, arrived at Bunker Hill in the early afternoon. They took up positions on the left flank of the main force on Breed's Hill, with 200 Connecticut men of Israel Putnam's regiment. "Old Put", as his men called him, shared command of some 1,000 militiamen with Colonel William Prescott of Massachusetts. Under cover of darkness the night before, they had constructed a 100-yard-square redoubt fortification atop Breed's Hill.

Regiments of Redcoats didn't begin arriving on the Charlestown Penninsula until 1:30 p.m. and General Howe didn't begin his attack until 3 p.m. Instead of a frontal attack as Colonel Prescott had expected, six regiments under General Howe made a flanking attack on John Stark's New Hampshire men. Stark hastily set up defenses down the sixty-foot slope of Breed's Hill to the banks of the Mystic River. Redcoats, led by the Royal Welsh Fusiliers, trotted down the beach towards Stark's makeshift barricade. Stark had placed a stick in the sand only 40-yards in front of his men, and ordered them not to fire until the Redcoats passed it. With bayonets poised, the British troops rushed forward. The New Hampshire men fired, reloaded, and as company after company charged them, they fired again. They repeated this until heaps of Redcoats lie dead or dying beside Stark's stick. The British retreated, leaving 96 of their men dead in the sand. "I never saw sheep lie as thick in the fold," said Stark. General Howe was shocked.

Further up the side of the hill, where New Hampshire and Connecticut farmers and frontiersmen crouched behind a stone wall and rail fence, some 400 Redcoats attacked. "Don't fire until you see the whites of their eyes," ordered "Old Put", and when the British were but 30-yards away, hammers clicked and muskets spit fire. When the smoke cleared, the Rebels could see hundreds of Redcoats retreating and hundreds more dead or wounded in the grass. General Howe wept. He regrouped the remainder of his army and attacked Stark and Putnam once more, only to be blasted from the beach and side of the hill again. Some of the British companies now had only six or seven men left standing. Howe sent for reinforcements.

The Americans suffered many casualties as well, and were dangerously low on ammunition. Colonel John Sullivan of New Hamsphire, who later became a General under Washington, had transported ox carts filled with gunpowder some 62 miles to Bunker Hill from Portsmouth. As General Howe regrouped and reinforced his Army, the Rebels were dipping into the last of Sullivan's gunpowder. Sullivan, the son of a Limerick school teacher who emigrated to Maine in 1730, had stolen the gunpowder at Portsmouth from the British fort six months before the battle. John's brother, Jim Sullivan, who was also fighting at Bunker Hill, became the most decorated soldier in the Revolutionary War and was later elected Governor of Massachusetts.

Among those killed in the initial fighting were two Irish-American Majors, Andrew McClary and Bill Moore. McClary, who stood 6' 6" tall was nicknamed, "The Giant Mick". In the ranks, those killed in Stark's Regiment included; Tom Collins, Dan Callahan, Tom Doyle, Dan McGrath, Bill Mitchell, Roger Cox, Joe Broderick, George Shannon, John Barrett, Bill McCrillis, and John Dillon, all were either born in Ireland, or were first generation Irish Americans. Of the Bedford, New Hampshire Company that took the brunt of the British attack on the rail fence, suffering many casualties, almost every man in it was Irish. Leading the Company was Dan Moore, second in command was Major John Goffe, under him was Captain Tom McLoughlin — all natives of Ireland.

With added regiments shipped over from Boston, General Howe was ready to attack again. This time, he marched his long red lines straight up Breed's Hill towards Prescott's redoubt-fort. The Massachusetts and Rhode Island men waited until the Redcoats were only 20-yards away before they opened fire. The red lines swayed. Those who didn't drop, turned and raced back down the hill. Howe regrouped and the Redcoats came at the Americans again, but by this time, most Colonials had fired their last round of ammunition. Many Redcoats fell, but the others pushed on, up and over the fortifications.

British Colonel Lord Rowden, who led the Irish-Redcoat Regiment, was first into Prescott's redoubt, where there was bloody hand-to-hand combat — the Redcoats using bayonets, the Americans using sticks, stones, and the butts of their muskets. The Americans retreated and the last to leave Breed's Hill were the remnants of the Charlestown militia — one of them was Irish-American Thomas Welsh, who went on to become America's first army surgeon. Although the British took the hill, they had paid dearly for it.

Of General Howe's 3,000 man regular army, 1,054 were casualties, including 89 British officers. The Americans lost 115 men, 304 wounded, and 30 captured. The British Army had never suffered such a slaughter! Bunker Hill was the bloodiest day of battle during the entire Revolutionary War. British General Gage, who had watched the battle from Boston, came to a painful conclusion: "The Rebels are not the despicable rable too many of us have supposed."

George Washington arrived at Army Headquarters at Cambridge, Massachusetts, shortly after the Battle Of Bunker Hill. With him came his Aide-De-Camp, Irish-born Colonel Stephen Moylan, whose brother was the Catholic Bishop of Cork. Their first job was to combine the militias from other Colonies with the New England militias, and to organize them into the United States Army. As Generals and commanding Colonels, Washington appointed ten who were born in Ireland and 18 who were Irish or Scotch-Irish Americans.

Following on Washington's heels into Cambridge was the strangest looking troop anyone in New England had ever seen. It was Irishman

Daniel Morgan from Derry, with 500 of his Virginia and Maryland frontiersmen. They had walked some 600 miles from Virginia to Massachusetts, wearing Indian moccasins. They were dressed in buckskins and floppy round hats, with feathers and porcupine quills decorating them. Sewn into the fronts of their shirts were the words, "Liberty or Death". They had tomahawks in their belts and they carried exceedingly long rifles. "A large proportion of them were Irishmen," writes Lossing in his Pictorial Field Book of the Revolution, "who were not very agreeable to the New Englanders, but a were a terror to the British." The riflemen were eventually sent to Vermont. With New England troops, including Ethan Allen's famous Green Mountain Boys, they pushed the British back into Canada as far as Quebec. Washington also sent Henry Knox into Vermont, where the Green Mountain Boys took British Fort Ticonderoga and Crown Point, confiscating over 100 cannons. Scotch-Irishman Knox had the seemingly impossible task of bringing the needed cannons to Boston.

Meanwhile, in Boston, 13,600 British soldiers and 6,600 residents had barricaded themselves into the Town. Washington, fearing that the British might break out and attack at any time, went so far as to have men released from New England jails to serve in the Army. Essex County records reveal that many men were thus recruited: "Ordered, December 5, 1775, that Ryan, now confined in Salem Gaol, be discharged, if he will enlist in the Army."

Most of the civilians who remained in Boston under British rule were Tories, true to King George, but according to General Howe, "some are Irish merchants residing in this Towne." These Irish merchants, in fact, "offered their services for the defense of this place," says the British General. "Under command of Captain James Forrest, they have armed and formed into a Company called, 'The Loyal Irish Volunteers,' and are distinguished by a white cockade."

Also opting to remain in Boston was a notorious thief from Dublin, Crean Brush. By devious means, he had earlier confiscated some 50,000 acres of land in Vermont, but General Gage liked him, and placed him in charge of all civilian supplies in Boston. As many frightened Tories emigrated to Canada or to England, unable to carry their valuable possessions with them they were turned over to Crean Bush for "safe keeping." After most of the Boston merchants had left town, Brush broke into their boarded up shops and stores, confiscating everything in them. Packing $100,000 worth of hand-picked ill-gotten valuables into the brigantine ELIZABETH, he planned to sail off to Ireland and live happily ever after. The brig ELIZABETH however, with the treasure and Brush aboard, was captured by an American privateer while she was leaving Boston Harbor. Crean Brush was put behind bars; 19 months later, dressed as a woman, he escaped jail and made his way to Vermont. There, he sadly discovered his lands had been confiscated by the American Rebels. Ethan Allen had married Crean Brush's daughter, and Crean couldn't understand how his own son-in-law could be so cruel as to take his property. Devistated, Brush used one of Allen's pistols to blow his own brains out.

Using oxen to drag cannons through the snow from Vermont to Dorchester, Massachusetts, Henry Knox and his men accomplished the near impossible. Knox chose Dublin born James Boies to set up a fortification on Dorchester Heights, which he accomplished in one night. Cannons were now aimed at Boston from the two highest hills overlooking the town, less than a mile from South Boston. "We were forced," as General Gage put it, "to quit the Towne." On Evacuation Day, March 17, 1776, 150 vessels carried British troops and Tories from Boston to Halifax. On that day, George Washington appointed John Sullivan, Officer-Of-The-Day, and the password for all sentries along the American front lines was "Boston," and the countersign was "Saint Patrick".

General Washington's confidential spy in New York, a "fashion-able clothier" named Hercules Mulligan, sent word to him that the British now planned to take New York and Vermont, including all Rebel strongholds along the Hudson River and Lake Champlain. They hoped to cut off New England from all other American Colonies. Mulligan, whose family hailed from County Mayo, supplied Washington with information on British troop movements throughout the Revolution. It was Hercules, with fellow Irishman Bill Mooney, who tore down the statue of King George and his horse at Bowling Green, New York on July 6, 1776 and then melted down the statue to make 40,000 bullets for the American Army.

In an attempt to stop the British from cutting off New England, Ethan Allen and his "Boys" charged into Canadian territory and tried to capture Montreal, but Allen was himself captured and shipped off to an English prison. Seth Warner then took command of the Vermont troops and did manage to take Montreal, but with Morgan's Riflemen and other New England troops under command of Irish-born General Richard Montgomery, they were defeated at Quebec and Montgomery was killed.

Burgoyne, with Redcoats, Tories, Hessians, and a detachment of Canadian Indians, swept down to New York and Vermont in 1777.

Warner and his men were routed at Hubbardton, Vermont, but John Stark and the New Hampshire troops, came to his rescue at Bennington on August 16, 1777. Upon meeting the British troops, Stark shouted to his 1,000-plus soldiers; "There my boys are your enemies, Redcoats and Tories. You must beat them, or Molly Stark sleeps a widow tonight." Beat them they did, killing over 200 and taking 600 prisoners. "It was the hottest battle I ever saw," commented Stark after the two hour conflict. As the Americans were about to celebrate their victory, a large force of British reinforcements showed up, and a second battle began which lasted until sundown, ending with a British retreat. For his efforts, John Stark was promoted to Brigadier General.

General Burgoyne with his main force of some 8,000 men was trying to cut off American troops from the Hudson River, but managed to march only 74 miles in 50 days, thanks to Daniel Morgan's "Merry Irishmen," as New Englanders were now calling them. The riflemen had been reinforced with Pennsylvania-Irish back-woodsmen, and now were 1,400 strong. They not only caused many of Burgoyne's Indian scouts to desert, but they burned bridges, felled trees, and made ingenious traps, delaying the Redcoats, and successfully cutting off their supply routes. Hoping to meet up with British General Howe's forces at Saratoga, Burgoyne and his Redcoats instead met up with a superior American force under the command of General Horatio Gates. The British held their own for over a week, but Morgan and his men met Burgoyne's main force in a bitter battle and forced the General to surrender. At this critical Battle of Bemis Heights on October 7th, it was Morgan's key rifleman, Timothy Murphy, who turned the battle in America's favor by killing British General Frazier, second in command to Burgoyne. Sharpshooter Murphy commented after the battle, "I shoots those with epaulettes rather than those who get paid sixpence per day." The Redcoats readily admitted that "Morgan's Irishmen with the twisted rifles are the greatest widow and orphan makers in the world." After the riflemen won many more battles for Washington, Daniel Morgan was promoted to Brigadier General. To his men, however, Morgan was, and always would be, their Irish Clan Chief, who blew loudly on a conch-shell like the great Irish Chief Brian Buru, as he led them into battle. To most Revolutionary War historians, his victory at Saratoga was the turning point of the War in favor of the Americans. It was also instrumental in bringing France into the War on America's side.

Colonel Archibald Campbell of the Royal 7th Highlanders, who was captured with his entire battalion in Boston Harbor and was taken prisoner, so admired the strange uniforms of Morgan's Rifleman, that he had one made for himself. Wearing it, he tried to escape from jail, but was recognized and recaptured. The lieutenant who caught the disguised Scotsman, said, "I think the Colonel would make a formidable Irish Rifleman." When the British and American Armys exchanged prisoners in New York in May of 1778, Colonel Campbell was exchanged for Vermont's Colonel, Ethan Allen.

Ethan Allen had been 32 months a prisoner-of-war in Canada and England. He had been treated miserably by the British, but he had one bright moment, when the prison ship he was on anchored at Cork, Ireland. The citizens of Cork took up a collection for the 50 American prisoners aboard the prison ship SOLEBAY, and "contributed largely to the relief and support of the prisoners," writes Allen. "It was so unexpected, so plentiful, and may I add, needful, it impressed on my mind the highest sense of gratitude." Two days later, the British captain confiscated the prisoners supplies, swearing that, "the damned American Rebels should not be feasted at this rate by the damned rebels of Ireland." Allen, however, states that, "I am confident, not only from the exercise of the well-timed generosity, but from a large acquaintance with gentlemen of this Irish nation, that as a people they excel in liberality and bravery."

When Ethan Allen says that he had "a large acquaintance" with Irishmen, he is more than likely referring to his "Green Mountain Boys", many of whom were born in Ireland or of Irish descent, and to his own family, including his wife, whose family came from Dublin. Allen's famous and fiery red headed nephew, Matthew Lyon, who was a Captain with the Green Mountain Boys, was born in Wicklow, Ireland. Matthew left his homeland for America as an indentured servant at age 15, after his father was hanged for plotting against the English. He was bought for twelve pounds by a Connecticut cattle merchant, but was able to buy his way out of servitude by selling two bulls. When Lyon then met up with Ethan Allen, he was working in a Connecticut coal mine. Matthew married Ethan's neice, and then, with the Allen clan, moved to the wilds of Vermont in 1769. With the Green Mountain Boys, he fought at Ticonderoga, Quebec, Bennington, and Saratoga, then left the American Army to help organize Vermont into a state. In 1796, he became a Congressman, known to his colleagues as, "The Lyon of Vermont." His political enemy William Corbett called him, "a wild animal caught in the bogs of Hibernia, and when a welp, was transported to America." When Lyon called John Adams "a madman", he was sent to jail for four months under the Sedition Act, but while in jail, Vermonters elected him to Congress again. When Thomas Jefferson and Aaron Burr locked horns for the Presidency of the United States, resulting in a tie vote, it was Matthew Lyon's one vote in Congress that elected Tom Jefferson. Lyon moved on to Kentucky, where he built gunboats for the American Navy, and for eight years served as a Congressman from that state. Then, at age 71, he moved to the Arkansas frontier and again was elected to Congress, but he died before he had a chance to serve again. "The Lyon Of Vermont" is probably the most outspoken and daring American Congressman who ever lived, and the only one who has represented three distinct districts in the U.S.

Matthew Lyon's predecessors in Congress, however, were a daring, rebellious lot in their own right. They met for the first time in Philadelphia, on September 5, 1774, but it was at their third meeting in June of 1776 that Thomas Jefferson wrote the Declaration of Independence, America's birth certificate. The Secretary of the Continental Congress, Charles Thomson, born in County Derry, Ireland, drafted the original document. The Declaration was ready for signatures on July 4, 1776, but only two men signed it that day, President of the Congress, John Hancock and Secretary Charles Thomson, two men who traced their roots to Ireland. The Declaration of Independence, as we know it, "engrossed on parchment," wasn't ready for signatures until August 2nd, 1776. By signing it, each man was sealing his death warrant, for, as they all well knew, if England should win the War, they would hang for treason. Twenty percent of the signers were either born in Ireland, or could trace their ancestry to the Emerald Isle.

John Hancock signed first, then 55 representatives of the thirteen Colonies added their names to the parchment. One of them, Thomas McKean, whose parents came from Ireland, didn't sign the Declaration until 1781, for he had gone off to join Washington's Army in 1776. The wealthiest of the signers was Irish Catholic Charles Carroll of Maryland. "I sign most willingly to the record of glory," he said as he scratched his name. "That will cost him a few million," laughed Tom Lynch, whose family came from Galway. He was an Irish-American, only 26 years old, and the youngest of the signers. Charles Carroll, with his "few million", outlived all the signers of the Declaration, dying in 1842 at age 105. New Hampshire's representative Matthew Thornton had emigrated to Wiscasset, Maine with his parents in 1717, from Limerick, Ireland and was a "distinguished physician of good humor", so said his Exeter neighbors. Besides Robert Treat Paine "O'Neill", and Scotch-Irishman George Read— signers Edward Rutledge, Charles Thomson, George Taylor, and James Smith were all born in Ireland. Taylor, after studying medicine in Ireland, became a Pennsylvania coal miner, married the boss' widow, and thereby became a wealthy man. Smith, who came from a very poor Irish family, raised the first volunteer Army Corps in Pennsylvania to fight the Redcoats.

"The Pennsylvania troops were the most effective fighting force in the Revolution," said General Henry Lee, second in command under Washington of America's armed forces. Over 20,000 men volunteered from Pennsylvania, placed under the command of Generals Wayne, Shea, Hand, O'Connor, Haslett, and Magase — all Irishmen. General Lee, who later became Governor of Virginia, wrote that, "Wayne's troops were known by the designation of the Line of Pennsylvania, whereas they might have been, with more propriety, called 'The Line of Ireland'. Bold and daring, they were impatient and refractory, and would always prefer an appeal to the bayonet to a toilsome march. They were singularly fitted for close and stubborn action, hand to hand in the center of the Army." A British commander wrote: "The Irish Line served everywhere and surrendered nowhere."

The "Irish Line", however, did not get along well with some of the Massachusetts and Connecticut troops. At Valley Forge, where, as General Lafayette said, "the unfortunate soldiers were in need of everything," a "stuffed Paddy" was made by some New England soldiers and paraded around the campground on March 17th, 1778. Washington's Irish soldiers, and especially those of Pennsylvania's Irish Line, didn't like this effigy of Saint Patrick. A great fist fight erupted, threatening a new revolution within the American Army. Washington rushed to the scene to break up the fight, calling the New England parade, "ridiculous and childish". The General asked the Irish soldiers to "point out the troublemakers", but the Irishmen refused. "Therefore," eyewitness to the incident Colonel McLane tells us, "Washington, with great promptness said, 'I too am a lover of Saint Patrick's Day, and must settle the affair by making all the Army keep the day.' He ordered extra drink to every man of his command and thus all made merry and were good friends." Throughout the remainder of the War, General Washington saw to it that the American Army celebrated Saint Patrick's Day.

The War for Independence not only united the American Colonies, but brought men of all nationalities and religions together in common cause, which helped to ease prior prejudices. The opening words of Thomas Jefferson's Declaration also helped eliminate frictions between various European groups that settled here — "We hold these truths to be self-evident: that all men are created equal, that they are endowed by their Creator with certain unalienable Rights, that among these are Life, Liberty, and the pursuit of Happiness . . .". The Irish, whose homeland had been plundered and pillaged for almost two centuries by the British, fought for life and liberty, and finally found happiness in their new homeland, here in America.

One of Morgan's "Merry Irishmen," and a soldier of Wayne's "Irish Line", who saw action in New England during the Revolutionary War. Sketches by Peter F. Copeland, "Uniforms of the American Revolution Coloring Book," Dover Publications, N.Y.

New Hampshire's Irish-American Generals John Sullivan and John Stark. Painting by Richard Staigg and drawing by Hannah Crowninshield, courtesy of the Essex Institute, Salem, MA.

VII
WHAT DOES YOUR IRISH NAME MEAN?

About 1,000 years ago, Ireland's greatest king, Brian Buru, had every family in the country assume a surname - so that family histories might be preserved. He was the first European leader to do so. Prior to that time, the Irish had names much like those adopted by the American Indians. Therefore, your family name could be "flying cloud", "dark warrior", "swift eagle", or maybe "sitting-bull". Translated from the ancient Irish language to English, you may be surprised, possibly even shocked, at what your surname really means. Most New England Irish-American family names are included here:

Ahern = Horse Owner

Atkins = Red Earth

Barrett = Bear

Barton = Grain Farmer

Bates = Stout

Biggs = Fat one

Bannon = Little White One

Barry = Spear

Berry = Fort Dweller

Begley = Little Rhymer

Bennett = Blessed

Bogan = Tender

Blaney = Lean Man

Boggs = Moist

Bourke = Stronghold

Boles = Tree Trunk

Bolger = Leather Maker

Bresnahan = Exporter

Broderick = Exciting

Brody = Thriller

Barnicle = Wild Goose

Butler = Care of Bottles

Brady = Spirited

Bowie = Victorious

Bowen = Well Born

Boyle = Vain Pledge

Boynton = From River Boyne

Bryant = Hill

Brogan = Sorrowful

Brennan = Raven

Briggs = Bridge Dweller

Broderick = Famous Ruler

Buckley = Pasture

Browder = Brother

Cadigan = Possessing Hundreds

Cain = Warrior

Call = Battle Mighty

Cahill = Battle Powerful

Callahan = Contention

Callaway = Gaellic Stranger

Cambell = Wry Mouth

Canning = Wolf Cub

Carter = Cart Driver

Canty = Satirist

Carey = Dark One

Carmichael = Castle of Michael

Carney = Winner

Carr = Black Hunter

Carrigan = Builder

Carroll = Stag

Carmody = Hunting Dog

Cashman = Curly Haired

Cassidy = Rapid

Casey = Watchful

Cawley = Wood Meadow

Clancy = Ruddy Warrior

Cloherty = Near A Stone

Clarke = Recorder

Cleary = Clerk

Cogan = Bowl

Cody = Assistant

Cochran = Confident

Comiskey = Confuser

Coffey = Battle Leader

Coleman = Hardness

Concannon = Soldier

Conant = Little Hound

Conby = Yellow Hound

Coen = Twin

Collins = Victory

Colvin = Ship

Conlon = Mighty

Connell = Powerful

Conley = Valorous

Conner = Meddlesome

Connery = Dog Keeper

Conroy = Plain Hound

Conway = Noisy

Costin = Constant

Conneally = Friendship

Coogan = Strife

Coughlon = Hooded Cloak

Cooley = Servant

Corbin = Chariott

Corcoran = Purple

Cotter = Cottage

Courtney = Drinking Cup

Cowen = Metal Worker

- 45 -

Cox = Neat Rooster
Coyle = Black Stranger
Cooney = Prosperity
Costello = Swift Footed
Crean = Sea Fairer
Cronin = Orange-Yellow
Crawley = Crow's Hill
Craven = Garlic
Creeden = Rocky Home
Creighan = Little Blind One
Crowley = Tough Hero
Cullen = Handsome Cub
Cullinan = Holly
Crotty = Hunchbacked
Cunniff = Black Hound
Cummings = From Flanders
Cunningham = Rabbit Farmer
Curran = Spear
Curley = Courageous
Curtis = Elegant Manners
Cushing = Firm Purpose
Dailey = Frequenting
Danahy = Human
Darrah = Black Oaks
Daugherty = Unfortunate
Davey = Beloved
Day = Good Luck
Deagan = Chosen
Deasy = People
Dever = Just Man
Devine = Minstrel
Devaney = Diving Sea Bird
Devitt = Son of David
Devlin = Black Pool
Dignan = Black Head
Dillon = Spoiler
Dineen = Brown
Doherty = Hurtful
Dolan = Black Hair
Donnelly = Brown Valor
Donahue = Brown Battler
Donlon = World Mighty

Donavan = Little Brown Bard
Dooley = Dark Hero
Dooling = Dark Defiant
Dorran = Alien
Dorcey = Door Keeper
Dowd = Black Complexion
Downey = Fort Dweller
Doyle = Swarthy Stranger
Drennan = Blackthorn
Driscoll = Interpreter
Duane = Little Black Person
Ducy = Black Choice
Duff = Black
Duncan = Brown Warrior
Dunn = Brown
Dunfey = Brown Soldier
Durkin = Gloomy One
Dunlevy = Son of Destroyer
Dwyer = Tawny Man
Egan = Fire
Ellis = Salvation
Ennes = Secluded
Enright = Unlawful
Fahey = Reasonable
Fallon = Governor
Farrell = Man of Science
Fanning = Fair
Farris = Better Choice
Feeney = Fighter
Fennessy = Fair Choice
Feeley = Chess Player
Ferguson = The Worthy
Fitzgerald = Son of Firm
Fitzgibbons = Little Pledge
Fitzmorris = Son of Dark One
Fitzpatrick = Son of Patrician
Flanagan = Red Man
Flattery = Son of Beautiful
Flavin = Blustering
Flannery = Red Eyebrows
Flynn = Ruddy Complexion
Fogerty = Exiled Man

Foley = Plunderer
Folan = Wolf
Forrestall = Game Keeper
Foy = Reasonable
Forbes = Fast
Ford = Defender
Flaherty = Bright Ruler
Gaffney = Calf
Gaugh = Cattle Rich
Garvey = Laughing
Gallagher = Foreign Helper
Galligan = Little White Person
Galvin = Bright
Garrity = Court Member
Garvin = Rough
Gegan = Racing Horse
Geary = Fighter
Gilligan = The Obediant Boy
Gilmartin = Living Boy
Gilmore = Great Boy
Gilroy = Red Boy
Gleason = Green
Glavin = Glutton
Glennon = Small Coat
Guiney = Prisoner
Grady = Noble
Hagan = Forest Man
Haggerty = Unjust
Halligan = Handsome Man
Halloran = Sea Stranger
Halpin = Money Changer
Haney = Bird
Hanlon = Great Hero
Hanraghan = Winner
Hannigan = Slow Man
Hannon = Delay
Harkins = Home Ruler
Harney = Fatherly
Hargan = Enchanted
Harrigan = Winning
Harrington = Tall Man
Hartigan = Stone

Hartnett = Battle Bear
Hassett = Strife
Hayden = Armored Man
Hayes = Enclosure
Healy = Skillful
Hearn = Horse Lord
Heffron = Eminent
Heneghan = Mean Bird
Hennessy = Despair
Herlihy = Underlord
Higgins = Ingenuity
Hoey = Horseman
Hogan = Young
Hoare = Grey Haired
Horan = Adverse
Hollahan = Loud Noise
Joyce = Joyful
Jennings = Gracious Gift
Jordan = Flowing Down
Keene = Quick
Kearney = Battle Won
Keating = Sense
Keefe = Gentle
Keegan = Heat
Keenan = Ancient
Kehoe = Jockey
Keiley = Companion
Keleher = Spouse Loving
Kelly = Contention
Kenneally = Learned Man
Kennedy = Favored
Kenny = Weary
Kern = Desire
Kernon = Village Owner
Kerr = Marsh Dweller
Kerrigan = Black One
Kirwan = Dark Skin
Kilcoyne = Gentle Youth
Kilduff = Black Youth
Kilgore = Goat Keeper
Kilroy = Red Haired
Kinney = From The Fire

Kinnsella = Head Stained
Kitto = Left Handed
Lackey = Footman
Lahey = Lord
Langdon = Long
Lannon = Mantle
Lavery = Spokesman
Lavin = Hand
Lawler = Mumbler
Leahy = Heroic
Leary = Cow Keeper
Lenihan = Cloaked
Lindsey = Son of Seaman
Looney = Jovial
Loughlin = Lake Dweller
Lonegan = Scoffer
McAdams = Son of Earth
McAndrews = Son of
    Manly One
McArdle = High Bravery
McAuliffe = Ancestor's Relic
McAvory = Yellow Haired
    Lad
McArthur = Son of Sailor
McBride = Servant of Brigid
McCabe = Hooded One
McCaffrey = God's Peace
McCahey = Cavalryman
McCall = Battle Chief
McCallum = Like A Dove
McCambridge = Immortal
McCarthy = Loving
McCartney = Little Bear
McClain = Servant of John
McCord = Son of Navigator
McCorkle = Thor's Kettle
McCoy = Son of Fire
McCrea = Son of Grace
McCue = Son of Burning
McCullough = Son of Boar
McCutcheon = Son of Spirit
McDaniel = World Mighty

McDermott = Free of Envy
McDonough = Strong Fighter
McDougall = Black Stranger
McDowell = Son of Blind
McGann = Son of Storm
McGee = Hot Flames
McGill = Son of Servant
MacGillycuddy = Devotee
    To Saint
McGinley = Son of Fair Valor
McGinnis = Son of One Choice
McGinty = Fair Snow
McGoldrick = Hot Tempered
McGovern = Son of Summer
McGonagle = Son of High
    Honor
McGarry = Son of Useful
McGuire = Son of Valiant
McHale = Son of Good
    Looking
McHugh = Son of Speaker
McShane = Son of Undefeated
Mackey = Virile
McKenna = Son of the Fire
McIrney = Church Steward
McIntyre = Wood Worker
McEvoy = Blond Lad
McEwen = Son of Well Born
McLellon = Little Wolf
McLeod = Ugly One
McMahon = Son of Bear
McManus = Son of Great One
MacMillan = Son of Bald One
McNally = Son of Poor Man
McNamara = Sea Hound
McNair = Son of Heir
McNaughton = The Pure One
McNeil = Son of Champion
McNichols = People's Victory
McNiff = Black Hound
McNutt = Sea Divinity
Madigan = Little Dog

Maher = Hospitable
Mahon = Bearlike
Mahoney = Grandson of Bear
Malloy = Proud One
Maloney = Devoted to Sunday
Mangin = Little Hairy One
Markey = Rider
Mead = Middle Grass
Meagher = Hospitable
Meehan = Honorable
Millikan = Little Bald One
More = Chief
Moran = Slave Seal
Morey = Majestic
Moriorty = Expert Seaman
Mulcahy = Warlike
Mullen = Dim
Mulvihill = Priest Helper
Muldoon = Commander of
    Garrison
Mullholland = Chief of
    Calends
Mullaney = Old Wise One
Mulligan = Little Bald One
Murdock = Of The Sea
Murphy = Sea Warrior
Murray = Beside The Sea
Murtaugh = Capable Seaman
Neary = Prosperous
Neely = High Honors
Nellis = The Champ
Nestor = Short Man of Halter
Nevin = Messenger
Nolan = Noble
Noonan = Small Beloved One
Nugent = Wet Meadow
O'Brien = The Author
O'Connell = High Powerful
O'Connor = Helping Warrior
O'Donnell = World Mighty
O'Hara = Sharp
O'Hare = Angry

O'Malley = Noble Chief
O'Meara = Merry
O'Neill = Military Prince
O'Rourke = Restless One
O'Shea = Orator
Orr = Pale
O'Toole = People Mighty
Phelan = Philospher
Pomeroy = Apple Orchard
Powers = Poor
Purcell = Young Pig Keeper
Paddon = Patrick
Quill = The Head
Queeney = Unspeaking
Quick = Heart
Quigley = Heart Escort
Quirk = The Knife
Quinlan = Free Friend
Quilty = Hard Headed
Quinn = Free Man
Rafferty = Stubborn
Rathe = Fort
Reagan = Councillor
Reardon = Royal Poet
Riordan = Umpire
Reilly = Impetous
Rooney = Ruddy Leader
Roach = Rock Dweller
Ronan = Little Seal
Ryan = Queen's Servant
Roayne = Red Seal
Shaughnessy = Elusive
Scully = School Man
Shanahan = Wise One
Sheehy = Peaceful
Shanley = Happiness
Shea = Orator
Scanlon = Joker
Spillane = Little Scythe
Sullivan = Black Eyed
Slattery = Bold
Sloane = Army Man

Spellman = Preacher
Scannell = Scandal
Sear = Sea Soldier
Sweeney = Peaceful One
Teeling = Small Duck
Twomey = A Sound
Tierney = Lordly
Tracy = Good Fighter
Tighe = A Bard
Talley = Quiet
Taft = Loved One
Tooley = Look Out
Tully = Small Hill
Timulty = Bulky
Tunney = Glittering
Walsh = A Welshman
Ward = Watchman
Welch = From Wales
Varley = Sharp Eyed Man
Whaley = Wolf Meadow
Whalen = Little Wolf
Whelton = Water Wheel
Wholley = Grandson of Proud
Wrenn = Spritely

(A Bibliography for this
book is available by writing
to Chandler-Smith Publish-
ing House.)

- 48 -